A
MULTI-SITE
CHURCH
ROADTRIP

The Leadership Network Innovation Series

A MULTI-SITE CHURCH ROADTRIP

EXPLORING THE NEW NORMAL

**GEOFF SURRATT, GREG LIGON,
AND WARREN BIRD**

ZONDERVAN.com/
AUTHORTRACKER
follow your favorite authors

We want to hear from you. Please send your comments about this book to us in care of zreview@zondervan.com. Thank you.

ZONDERVAN

A Multi-Site Church Roadtrip
Copyright © 2009 by Geoff Surratt, Greg Ligon, and Warren Bird

This title is also available as a Zondervan ebook. Visit www.zondervan.com/ebooks.

This title is also available in a Zondervan audio edition. Visit www.zondervan.fm.

Requests for information should be addressed to:

Zondervan, *Grand Rapids, Michigan 49530*

Library of Congress Cataloging-in-Publication Data

Surratt, Geoff, 1962–
    A multi-site church roadtrip : exploring the new normal / Geoff Surratt, Greg Ligon, and Warren Bird.
        p. cm. — (Leadership network innovation series)
    Includes bibliographical references and index.
    ISBN 978-0-310-29394-1 (softcover)
    1. Church growth. 2. Church facilities — Planning. 3. Church management. I. Ligon, Greg, 1962 – II. Bird, Warren. III. Title.
    BV652.25.S86 2009
    254 — dc22   2009015940

Interior design by Mark Sheeres

Printed in the United States of America

09 10 11 12 13 14 • 20 19 18 17 16 15 14 13 12 11 10 9 8 7 6 5 4 3 2 1

CONTENTS

No longer primarily for megachurches, multi-site campuses range from a few dozen people meeting in a neighborhood clubhouse to thousands of attenders in a brand-new church building.

More people are approaching the issue as "both-and" rather than "either-or." One of the big surprises is how many church planters have embraced multi-site.

A multi-site church is either a church *with* multiple sites or a church *of* multiple sites. Making the all-important shift from *with* to *of* brings a significant change to the culture of the church. This subtle shift transforms the core identity of the church and will affect everything you do.

Choosing the right location for the next campus is one of the most difficult decisions for a multi-site church. Each church's vision, values, and context help it shape the strategy that will have the greatest kingdom impact.

Multi-site churches are transforming their communities by contextualizing their service and outreach to the unique needs of each location.

13. MULTIPLIED, MULTIPLE LEADERS
Good leadership is always the key to healthy, growing churches. That need multiplies and increases in multi-site churches. Effective multi-site churches have an established culture and well-developed strategies for reproducing and growing biblical leaders.

14. ARE YOU SURE THIS ISN'T A SIN?
While some say going multi-site is simply a new opportunity to obey Jesus' great commission, others raise cautions. Are there biblical values that might be lost or weakened by the multi-site growth model?

15. GRANDCHILDREN ALREADY?
Many churches are moving from addition to multiplication as secondary campuses begin launching campuses of their own. This new wave of "grandchildren" increases the challenges of DNA transfer.

EPILOGUE: PREDICTIONS OF WHAT'S NEXT.
The multi-site revolution is still mushrooming, a new normal is emerging, and the implications are rich for how the next generation will see and do church.

INTRODUCING THE ROADTRIP

Greg, Warren, and I (Geoff) met in 2003 at Leadership Network's first Multi-Site Churches Leadership Community gathering. As director of that community, Greg had assembled from around the country twelve churches experimenting with the relatively new concept of being one church meeting in multiple locations. Warren's role in the community was to capture what the churches in the group were learning and to share that knowledge with other churches around the country. I came as a member of the team from Seacoast Church in Charleston, South Carolina. At the time, Seacoast met in five locations and was desperate to learn from other pioneers how to make this new paradigm work.

Over the group's two-year life span, Greg and Warren discovered a ground swell of interest from churches wanting to know more about doing ministry in multiple locations under one umbrella organization. Warren's multi-site articles were downloaded by thousands of leaders across North America, and Greg heard from dozens of pastors whose churches were moving to a multi-site model. The two of them began framing a book about this "multi-site revolution" that seemed to be mushrooming. I came on board to provide insight from what we were doing at Seacoast, as a thread to be woven through the book. As my brother Greg, senior pastor at Seacoast, often says, "Everyone is good for something, even if it is to be a bad example." My job in helping write *The Multi-Site Church Revolution* was to provide that example.

Our goal was to provide an overview of the multi-site movement and to offer handles for churches to hold on to as they moved toward the multi-site model. *The Multi-Site Church Revolution* defines a multi-site church as "one church meeting in multiple locations — different rooms on the same campus, different locations in the same region, or in some instances different cities, states, or nations. A multi-site church shares a common vision, budget, leadership, and board."[1] In that first book, we identify five basic models of multi-site churches: video venues, regional campuses, teaching teams, partnerships, and low-risk models. We also explore specific models of each. In addition, we drill down on issues such as finding opportunity, launching successfully, designing a workable support structure, developing the leadership needed, and funding the expansion to additional campuses.

Ready for a Roadtrip?

In the three years since *The Multi-Site Church Revolution* was published, the revolution has literally exploded. Practically every major city in America now has several multi-site churches, and many smaller communities are experiencing the same phenomenon. Greg, Warren, and I have each had the chance to visit dozens of multi-site churches across the country and to experience the latest innovations in the movement.

We want to share those fresh ideas with you. Our first thought was to load everyone into buses for a cross-country roadtrip, but when we looked at the cost of renting all those buses, we decided to take you on a virtual roadtrip instead. On this simulated excursion, we'll be "visiting" a variety of multi-site churches all over America. We'll tour each church, dive into what the people there have learned, and take a few side trips to churches doing similar ministry.

When visiting a church today, few are surprised if the worship service includes signing for the hearing impaired, a short dramatic skit, or electronic projection of the Scripture reading for the day — all innovations in recent decades. Likewise, we believe the day is rapidly approaching when few will find it unusual for a church to offer simultaneous worship services in a sanctuary, gym, and chapel (multiple venues) or even in the original church building, a public school across town, a theater adjacent to the nearby university, *and* the clubhouse of a retirement community thirty miles away (multiple campuses).

Multi-Site as the New Normal

During one of my most recent multi-site church visits, I (Warren) made a big mistake. I was in Long Island, New York, to check out Shelter Rock Church, which we'll profile in chapter 11.

I had assumed I was at the church's main campus. I was wrong, but nothing clued me in to my misunderstanding, which speaks volumes about how far multi-site has come.

The congregation seemed well established in the facility, which had the date 1952 on its cornerstone. The worship was vibrant, and the congregation offered a wide range of ministry, from children's programming to community service options. The sanctuary had been modernized in recent years, and most of the two hundred seats were delightfully full. The bulletin listed the morning's teaching pastor, a couple of staff members associated with the campus, and volunteer leaders of various ministries.

All these indicators led me to guess that this must be the main campus, and the other site—which I planned to visit also—was the satellite campus.

I was wrong, but I didn't learn that until a subsequent weekend when I worshiped at the other campus. I found that it too was in a long-established but modernized building. It too had vibrant worship, with 250 full seats plus a 50-seat video venue in the fellowship hall. And it also had great, live teaching, with a bulletin listing the pastor's name, a few staff, and volunteer ministry leaders, just like the other campus.

When I had visited the other Shelter Rock campus (which is technically their "first" campus), I introduced myself to the man sitting next to me, who happened to be a reporter for the *New York Times*. He had no interest in whether this was the first or second campus, or even the third or fourth (which they don't have yet, but they're exploring). He had been sent to cover this church for a story on how people seem to be flocking to churches for spiritual help during times of national economic turmoil. His subsequent article was quite positive. It opened by referencing a man who had lost his job and who looked to "a more personal relationship with God" to give him the anchor he and his family needed through some tough times.[2]

The *New York Times* article gave only a six-word reference to the fact that this was one church in two locations.

Imagine that! The two-campus idea is either so normal that it wasn't worth mentioning, or else—more likely—the reporter found the "crush of worshipers packing the small church" (his words) far more newsworthy.

We think that's the way it should be. For most churches, multi-site is a means to an end: helping people grow closer to God. Most multi-site churches don't make one campus the main deal and give the other venues or campuses second-class or overflow status. (For that reason, we avoid the terms "main campus" and "first campus" in this book.) Multi-site can work in churches of many sizes, not just megachurches. And multi-site is normal enough that the *Times* could summarize it in a six-word explanation, noting in passing that Shelter Rock Church also has "a satellite church in nearby Syosset."

Making Churches More Nimble

Yet in other ways the multi-site idea is something newsworthy, and not just because the three of us got to visit lots of multi-site churches and eat lots of good food with their pastors. It's newsworthy because it's being introduced everywhere.

A newspaper's front-page headline summarized in one sentence a major advantage of becoming multi-site. It read, "Instead of Bricks and Mortar, Allison Church Invests in Technology to Create More Space for Worshippers."[3]

The article explained that Allison Church in Moncton, New Brunswick, is now in two places at once on Sunday mornings. Or as the church's motto reads, "One church, different locations."

David Morehouse is lead pastor at this church serving a city with a population of 125,000. Nowadays, for its 11:00 a.m. services—the most popular of the church's three Sunday services—many more people can attend, because Allison Church meets simultaneously at two church buildings in the same town. Before the new arrangement, the 11:00 a.m. service threatened to violate fire codes every week, with 300 to 350 people packing into the seats.

While some churches, such as Shelter Rock, do multiple-site worship through in-person teaching teams, Allison Church does its teaching through video technology. The second-site worship service begins with on-site live music, and then a campus pastor introduces the morning message, recorded at an earlier service that same weekend. The location that plays the video, which alternates between the two campuses, lacks any sense of a glorified overflow room or of being second-class. People "don't feel like they're being gypped or that they're missing out," the pastor told the newspaper. Both sites are just as personal in the culture they convey. "Relationships are what hold churches together," he affirmed, and in moving to its new approach, the church took care not to violate that core value.

The multi-site approach at Allison Church saved huge amounts of money compared with an expansion of their existing facility. The video technology cost them less than 5 percent of the estimated cost of an addition. "Rather than having to build more infrastructures on one site, some churches are becoming more nimble and mobile," the pastor said. Plus, this approach enables the church to reach more people.

In Moncton, community response to the new venture was rather positive. Soon enough, most people had accepted the idea that it's normal for a ninety-year-old church like Allison to hold worship services at two (or more) locations under the umbrella of a single identity, with a unified budget and board and the same senior leader.

Not a Fad

Both Shelter Rock Church and Allison Church helped pioneer multi-site in their towns, but they won't lack company if present trends continue. According to Leadership Network's data collection and our own estimations, those trends include the following:

▶ On a typical Sunday in 2009, some five million people—almost 10 percent of Protestant worshipers—attend a multi-site church in the United States or Canada.

▶ At least forty-seven U.S. states, and Canada's four largest provinces, have congregations that describe themselves as one church in many locations.

▶ Leaders at some forty-five thousand churches are "seriously considering adding a worship service at one or more new locations or campuses in the next two years," according to a 2008 random survey of Protestant pastors conducted by Lifeway Research.[4]

▶ From 2006 through 2008, nearly seven hundred churches attended Leadership Network–sponsored conferences on how to become, or improve as, a multi-site church.

▶ More than 20,000 documents have been downloaded from Leadership Network's website of free resources for anyone interested in the multi-site approach, a number that started with 2,089 in 2003 and has increased steadily.

▶ Some 37 percent of megachurches reported being multi-site in 2008, up dramatically from 27 percent in 2005. Interestingly, average seating capacities in American megachurches grew only minimally between 2005 and 2008 (from 1,709 to 1,794), while the churches grew in overall average attendance from 3,585 to 4,142—doing so by becoming multi-site and also by increasing the average number of services offered each weekend, from 4.4 in 2005 to 5.3 in 2008.

Granted, the multi-site movement was initially championed and popularized by megachurches, but one of the messages of this book is that you don't have to be a megachurch to go multi-site. We've visited enough churches of all sizes, and heard accounts of still more, to affirm with confidence that a healthy church with regular attendance (not membership) of two hundred or more can often become multi-site with an outcome that greatly increases the number and quality of disciples it makes. Healthy churches with attendances of less than two hundred can do certain forms of multi-site with good success, as both this book and our previous *Multi-Site Church Revolution* underscore.

> You don't have to be a megachurch to go multi-site.

In short, the multi-site phenomenon is growing dramatically among churches of all sizes, bringing it soon enough to every city, every denomination, and every style of ministry.

Innovation Isn't New for Churches

In his groundbreaking book *The Diffusion of Innovations*, respected professor Everett Rogers says that in any innovation, from the idea stage to widespread adoption, there are five types of adopters: innovators, early adopters, early majority, late majority, and laggards (which many today describe more kindly as reluctants). We have seen these same practices at work as the idea of a multiple-location church has spread across the country.

During the last ten years, various innovators—churches that were regionally known at best—began trying different ways of being one church in more than one location. They included Community Christian Church (Naperville, Illinois), New Life Christian Fellowship (Virginia Beach, Virginia), and Eastern Star Missionary Baptist Church (Indianapolis, Indiana). Other pioneers, such as North Coast Church (Vista, California) and LifeChurch.tv (Edmond, Oklahoma), added a video component, which proved to be a key technology piece to the puzzle. Other churches, such as Christ the King Community Church (Mount Vernon, Washington), pioneered the idea of geographic irrelevance, replicating just as handily in an overseas country as in a next-door town. This proved to be another key component to what we see today.

Next, a number of opinion-leader churches got into the water. A lot of them stepped in cautiously at first, but once both feet were wet, they began swimming in a very noticeable way. Many of the leaders of these churches became spokespeople for the movement. They are actually the early adopters of others' practices, but they add money, muscle, and influence to the movement. Professor Rogers would say they helped begin the diffusion of the innovation.

> This book's big thread is a story of how pioneers and innovators in several micromovements helped (and continue to help) other opinion leaders see it, get it, and do it.

This book's big thread is a story of how pioneers and innovators in several micromovements helped (and continue to help) other opinion leaders see it, get it, and do it.

We believe that the Holy Spirit is behind the multi-site movement and that, in keeping with Everett Rogers' pattern of how innovation is diffused, it is only just beginning. The time line on page 17 illustrates the movement's diffusion pathway.

While "multi-site" is the dominant term for the idea of one church in multiple locations, many churches are personalizing the idea with phrases of their own. Willow Creek Community Church (South Barrington, Illinois) and Saddleback Church (Lake Forest, California) call their various locations regional campuses; Upper Arlington Lutheran Church (Columbus, Ohio) calls their three campuses a church of communities. Community Christian Church (Naperville, Illinois) calls their locations poly-sites. Other congregations call them everything from satellites to house churches to mission campuses.

> The idea of one church in two or more locations is anything but a cloning formula.

So the idea of one church in two or more locations is anything but a cloning formula. Churches approach it in different ways. The trigger moments differ that cause churches to explore the multi-site idea. One size and one approach still don't fit all for multi-site.

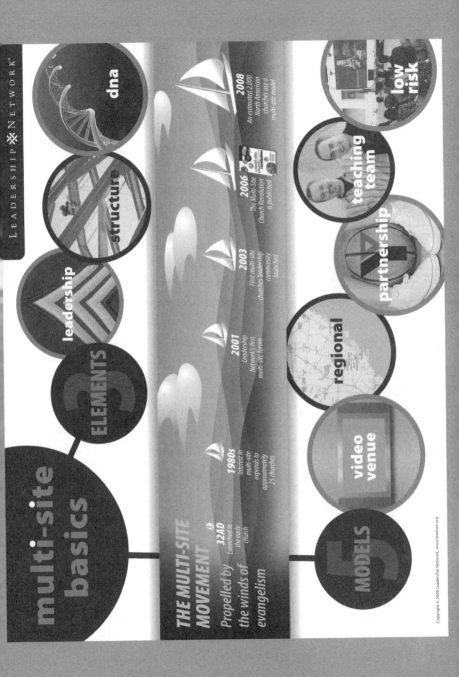

LEADERSHIP NETWORK®

multi-site basics

dna

structure

leadership

3 ELEMENTS

THE MULTI-SITE MOVEMENT

Propelled by the winds of evangelism

32AD
launched in the early church

1980s
Interest in multi-site expands to approximately 25 churches

2001
Leadership Network's first multi-site forum

2003
First multi-site churches leadership community launched

2006
The Multi-Site Church Revolution is published

2008
An estimated 2,000 North American churches use a multi-site model

low risk

teaching team

partnership

regional

video venue

5 MODELS

But the bottom line is that the public face of the North American church is changing. Yesterday most churches offered only one service at one time. Today most offer multiple services at multiple times. Tomorrow—or perhaps later this afternoon—it will be quite common for churches to offer multiple venues and multiple campuses as well.

The Next Big Thing in Religion?

Sometimes national newspapers and magazines look for the big scoop for their religion column by identifying something as the next big thing in religion. We don't think multi-site fits that billing. It's really not new. Multi-site is all about the two-thousand-year-old challenge of reaching people and making disciples, just with a different wrapper on the package. Long ago horse-drawn carriages became horseless carriages, today known as automobiles. The look changed, but ultimately they're both about transportation. Likewise, one-location churches are becoming multiple-location churches, but they're still about helping people find new life through Jesus Christ.

> Multi-site is all about the two-thousand-year-old challenge of reaching people and making disciples, just with a different wrapper on the package.

We want you to make your own decision by coming along with us to many of the dozens of multi-site churches we've experienced firsthand. By taking you to these churches, we hope to develop for you the picture of multi-site diffusion. So if you're looking for creative ways to reach new people for Christ or to take "church" to where

> We want you to make your own decision by coming along with us to many of the dozens of multi-site churches we've experienced firsthand.

the people are, join us for an insider's tour of the kind of churches we're all certain to see a lot more of very soon.

In this book, we'll take you to more than a dozen states, covering a wide range of church sizes and church families. Each chapter will have a different emphasis, and many will also reference the various kinds of food we enjoyed on our visits. Go grab something to eat so you won't get hungry. Then buckle your seat belt, and let's go!

SEACOAST CHURCH

Mount Pleasant,
South Carolina

SEACOAST CHURCH

FAST FACTS

Church vision ▶	***To help people become devoted followers of Christ.***
Year founded ▶	***1988***
Original location ▶	***Mount Pleasant, South Carolina***
Lead pastor ▶	***Greg Surratt***
Teaching model for off-sites ▶	***Primarily video/DVD***
Denomination ▶	***Nondenominational***
Year went multi-site ▶	***2002***
Number of campuses ▶	***13***
Number of weekly services ▶	***33***
Worship attendance (all physical sites) ▶	***10,000***
Largest room's seating capacity ▶	***1,300***
Internet campus? ▶	***Yes***
International campus? ▶	***No***
Internet address ▶	***www.seacoast.org***

Note: All data for the Fast Facts tables at the start of each chapter are from mid-2009.

No longer primarily for megachurches, multi-site campuses range from a few dozen people meeting in a neighborhood clubhouse to thousands of attenders in a brand-new church building.

In order for us to experience the full range of multi-site diversity, the first stop on our roadtrip will be Seacoast Church, originally located among the old live oaks and Civil War – era plantations of Charleston, South Carolina. We'll begin our visit a few miles outside of Charleston, in the small town of Manning, population 3,947.

It's easy to miss Manning when you are driving up I-95 through the rural surroundings of South Carolina. On my first visit to Manning, I (Geoff) would have easily passed the expressway exit if I hadn't seen the prominent Shoney's billboard on the highway. A local pastor had invited me to meet him at that restaurant to discuss the possibility of his church being adopted by Seacoast. Though I was excited about the discussion, I was also secretly hoping they would be having an all-you-can-eat seafood day.

After I met with the pastor and we enjoyed some excellent hot cross buns, the two of us agreed that Manning would be a great place for Seacoast's next multi-site experiment, opening a campus in a small town. At the time, Seacoast was drawing almost ten thousand people every weekend. The campuses were spread across twelve locations throughout North Carolina, South Carolina, and Georgia.

But what would happen if we opened a campus in a town like Manning, where the entire municipal population was only half the attendance of Seacoast? Six weeks later we found out, when Seacoast Manning was born. Soon about eighty people were gathering from across Clarendon County each weekend to worship in a rented community college auditorium. From the beginning, exciting things were happening. One woman started bringing her brother to the church.

"He's now actively exploring areas of faith, church, and a relationship with Christ, none of which were really open for discussion before the Manning campus opened," she said. My Shoney's acquaintance, who became the campus pastor, still shares stories about friends and family who are attending. "The opening of the Manning campus was an answer to so many prayers," he says.

An hour south of Manning is Summerville, a suburb of Charleston. Affordable housing and proximity to Charleston has led to a great deal of growth in Summerville, but it has still managed to maintain a small-town-America feel. The biggest event each year is the Azalea Festival, during which people come from all over the county to see flowers and eat fried things on a stick. Seacoast started a Summerville campus on Easter Sunday 2004 in a senior citizen community center, and every Sunday since that opening, campus pastor Phil Strange and his wife, Sherri, have stood at the door after services and hugged people leaving the building.

The campus then relocated to its own facility, and they saw weekend attendance jump from six hundred to over twelve hundred. Pastor Phil has maintained the small-town feel, but he is no longer able to hug everyone who walks out the door. Though it's not for lack of trying!

Fifteen minutes east of Summerville on I-26 is North Charleston, recently named the seventh most dangerous city in America. In the heart of North Charleston, on one of the most crime-ridden streets in the city, you'll find the Seacoast Dream Center. Every Sunday morning, six hundred people from the community gather in a little traditional church building for worship that sounds a little like David Crowder, a little like Al Green, and a little like tobyMac. The crowd is an eclectic mix of African Americans, first-generation Hispanic immigrants, and blue-collar whites. Campus Pastor Sam Lesky has created a family atmosphere for people who have never known what it is to be cared for and loved unconditionally. In the midst of all the crime and urban decay, God is changing people's lives daily.

Jumping back on the highway, we travel to Mount Pleasant, the home of Seacoast's original campus—fifteen minutes by car but a world away economically. Every weekend approximately 5,000 middle-class suburbanites gather in three on-campus venues featuring simultaneous worship experiences. One venue is an auditorium that seats 1,300 and features contemporary worship. Another venue is a traditional 300-seat chapel featuring acoustic music sprinkled with a mix of hymns and modern worship songs. The third venue is a rugged 450-seat warehouse with fog, moving lights, and guitar-driven worship.

All these venues are joined by a large lobby that resembles a shopping mall and features a full-service coffee bar and a large bookstore. Because of the variety of venues and the size of the crowd, attenders can come and go anonymously, or if they wish, they can join one of the dozens of ministries or hundreds of small groups that are part of Seacoast Church.

One Size Doesn't Fit All

Being one church with multiple locations has allowed Seacoast to grow larger *and* smaller at the same time. In the past seven years, Seacoast has seen its overall weekend attendance grow from three thousand to over ten thousand. At the same time, people are attending Seacoast campuses of eighty, one hundred, three hundred, eight hundred, one thousand, and five thousand people.

Some people appreciate the anonymity of the large congregation. They like the safety of being able to blend into the crowd without fear of being pointed out. They want to be able to move at their own pace toward a relationship with Jesus, and the huge congregation gives them that opportunity. A smaller crowd would be intimidating.

> Being one church with multiple locations has allowed Seacoast to grow larger *and* smaller at the same time.

A larger congregation can also offer a larger palette of ministries. For example, Seacoast's largest campus offers at every service a "One by One" ministry for special-needs children. While smaller campuses may see the need for such a ministry, they often don't have the room or the volunteers to make it happen. For some people bigger really is better.

Other people crave the intimacy available in a small-church atmosphere. They want to go where everybody knows their name (to borrow from the theme song for *Cheers*). They want people to notice when they are missing, to know their children's names, to ask them about their job. People in Seacoast's smaller congregations like the fact that they know their campus pastor and that the campus pastor knows them. While a smaller campus doesn't have state-of-the-art facilities or a large selection of specialized ministries, it can often offer closer connections and more intimate relationships.

Why the Variety Pack Works for Seacoast

Having multiple campuses of multiple sizes in multiple cities and states certainly isn't for everyone. Many multi-site churches, such as Willow Creek in the Chicago area, try to replicate the ministries of the original site as closely as possible each time they open a new campus, although their downtown Chicago site did also take on an urban flair. When Prestonwood Church in Greater Dallas decided to expand to more than one location, they first purchased 127 acres in Prosper (an exurb about seventeen miles north of Plano) and built a new building that somewhat rivaled their original

> Having multiple campuses of multiple sizes in multiple cities and states certainly isn't for everyone.

site. Central Christian Church in the Phoenix area and Southeast Christian Church in Greater Louisville have had a lot of success with similar large-campus satellite strategies.

Seacoast, however, has purposely decided to grow larger and smaller at the same time. As a staff, we are constantly asking how we can reach more people with the gospel in a variety of contexts and help them grow in their faith, and for us the answer includes many different sizes and formats. We have found several advantages in the variety pack approach to multi-site campuses:

1. A Variety of Opportunities to Volunteer

The complexity of having several campuses offers a new set of opportunities for volunteer leaders. We have several CEOs, CFOs, and small business owners who volunteer to help us figure out the corporate side of organizing a diverse set of church campuses. While these individuals might not be fulfilled serving the church by handing out bulletins or changing diapers, they eagerly dive into helping us figure out how to leverage the resources God has given for the maximum kingdom impact. The challenge of managing a large organization spread across three states allows these men and women to use their God-given gifts in ways that go beyond the marketplace. When the economy began to tank in recent years, we were especially thankful to have high-capacity volunteers such as these to help us steer the ship.

We also have opportunities for engineers who like to figure out traffic patterns. The parking lot at our Summerville campus has only one entrance and one exit. On some weekends the parking lot has to be turned over with only fifteen minutes between services. Engineers love this kind of stuff. Summerville has cones and ropes and people wearing orange vests and waving batons in every direction, and they do an amazing job.

We also have a wide variety of service opportunities for anyone who likes to work with children. We have nurseries with as few as two babies at a time, and rooms with as many as one hundred children. We utilize teachers and small group leaders and baby rockers and door monitors. Whatever a person's gifting, experience, or availability, there is always a place for him or her to experience the joy of serving at a Seacoast campus.

2. Artist Development at Various Levels of Skill

Having multiple campuses of multiple sizes allows Seacoast to develop artists of every skill level. Each week, Seacoast uses as many as twenty different bands across all the campuses. We have beginning drummers who are just learning how to hold the sticks playing for their junior high classmates, as well as professional guitar players home from a recent tour playing for thousands of people. When we have tryouts for new musicians, the answer is always "Yes, we can use you." We find that some people are ready to play for a big venue, some are ready to learn in a smaller environment, and some need to play in a youth band without an amplifier while they learn their instrument. The exciting part of having so many bands is that there is always an opening for new musicians.

> When we have tryouts for new musicians, the answer is always "Yes, we can use you."

3. Leadership Development at a Wide Range of Levels

Seacoast's multiple-size, multiple-location structure is also great for developing new leaders. There is always a place for leaders to grow, and there is no ceiling on our capacity for growing them. Small group leaders can become coaches. Coaches can become directors. Directors can become pastors. Pastors can become campus pastors. Campus pastors can become senior pastors. (And to give them an alternative to sponsoring a takeover coup in order to do that, we will help them plant their own church through the Association of Related Churches [www.relatedchurches.com].)

Another advantage for leadership development is the variety of opportunities to lead. Without ever leaving Seacoast, a leader can experience working in a megachurch environment, being on staff of a medium-size congregation, and leading a small church.

A church does not have to be our current size to provide the opportunity for leadership development, of course. From our opening moments as a much smaller church, we've tried to be a place that empowers God's people for ministry as they use their spiritual gifts and grow by serving.

4. Diversification into Multiple Cultures

For the first fourteen years of its existence, Seacoast was a predominately white, upper-middle-class congregation. We were a reflection of the community around us, even though some of our people drove in from other communities. All of our ministries, our music, and our messages were aimed at people who looked, talked, and lived just like "us."

When we went multi-site, our racial and socioeconomic makeup changed. One of the healthiest side effects of having multiple locations has been the expansion of our vision beyond the community around us.

> When we went multi-site, our racial and socioeconomic makeup changed.

But this benefit hasn't come without challenges. Recently our senior pastor included in his message a major point about paying as much attention to the Bible as you do to your BlackBerry. As you might expect, this struck a chord with our overly connected, stressed-out soccer moms and small business owners. But the urban poor in our congregation were just confused—or irritated at an implied lifestyle. The only blackberry many of them had experience with was the pie they ate for dessert last week.

Not Just Seacoast

This variety pack approach for multi-site—big *and* small, with diverse volunteer needs, broad leadership development opportunities, and culturally diverse membership—seems to be the normal path for many churches that become one church in many locations. When the multi-site revolution first started, many of the conversations were about embracing a franchise model like that of Starbucks: do all campuses and venues need the same look, down to the napkins, in order to keep the DNA of the church they're part of?

Today most multi-site churches are trading the Starbucks model for a tour through Legoland. Like Legoland, they are able to showcase a tremendous variety of sizes and designs, but it's still evident that everything is built from the same blocks.

As an example of this new model, let's consider New Direction Christian Church. They have two campuses: one in an urban section of Memphis, Tennessee, and the other in the growing suburb of Collierville, twenty minutes east of the city. The original urban campus seats 3,000 in a boxlike converted anchor store of a shopping outlet. The suburban campus, converted from a former grocery store, is rectangular, with the 525 seats only eight rows deep at any point. While both campuses are over 90 percent African American, the city (or Memphis) campus has more of an urban, younger flair, while the suburban campus, in keeping with its neighborhood, draws more families and a higher economic class. The city campus, which occupies twenty-two acres, has signs and banners all over the property. The suburban campus, due to zoning restrictions, puts signage only on its building, and quite limited signage at that.

> Most multi-site churches are trading the Starbucks model for a tour through Legoland.

Yet the Lego-feel culture is unmistakable between the two campuses. Dr. Stacy Spencer, senior pastor, preaches live at both campuses on Sundays and during midweek services. The Collierville campus pastor is also regularly visible at the Memphis campus. The programming of the campuses is similar, as is the heartbeat and overall sense of mission. New Direction may be reaching two different groups of people in two very different communities, but they've figured out how to truly be one church in two locations.

Staying on the Same Page

Indeed, a church with campuses of different sizes and locations often struggles with a basic question of unity: "What makes us *one* church?" From a structural standpoint, all the campuses might share one leadership configuration, one budget, and one mission, but on a practical basis, what do they have in common? Does every campus need to sing the same songs each weekend? Should each campus use the same color coffee cups? Can each children's ministry director choose a different curriculum?

After struggling for many years with these challenges, Seacoast finally drafted something called an IPOD (a concept we first heard from Jim Kuykendall at Cross Timbers Community Church, a multi-site congregation in Argyle, Texas). This has helped us keep all of our campuses on the same page while giving each the freedom to create a unique flavor of Seacoast for their community. For our church, IPOD is an acronym (not a portable music player). It stands for Initial, Priority, Optional, and Discouraged. The IPOD standards were drafted by a team of staff members and volunteers from each ministry and approved by Seacoast's directional leadership team.

- ▶ *Initial.* These are the nonnegotiable standards that every Seacoast campus must have in place from the first day it opens. We try to keep these standards to the bare minimum, to ease the burden on a brand-new campus. To be in the Initial list, a standard must be equally applicable to a campus of fifty or a campus of five thousand. Initial standards for children's ministry, for instance, include what classes will be provided and what curriculum will be used in each class.
- ▶ *Priority.* These are standards that a campus needs to implement within its first year of existence. Many of these are difficult to put into practice on your first weekend, but a campus can grow into them. Priority items for small groups, for example, include quarterly community outreach events and bimonthly huddles for small group coaches.
- ▶ *Optional.* These are ideas that might be great at one campus but might not work well at another. One of the challenges of

various-size campuses is that the smaller ones think they have to do everything the larger or more established campuses do. This is impractical and can actually keep a smaller campus from growing.

▶ *Discouraged.* These are practices that are strongly discouraged (okay, not allowed) at Seacoast campuses. Like the Initial category, this is a category we keep to a minimum. The IPOD standards are intended to be guides that allow freedom, not rules that discourage creativity. For example, our children's ministries are discouraged from having volunteers serve alone in a room and from combining different age groups into one class.

IPODs have allowed Seacoast to remain one church of many campuses, while encouraging each of the individual campuses of many sizes to contextualize the Seacoast model so it matches the unique makeup of their community. Seacoast has been able to grow larger and smaller at the same time without losing its distinct identity.

> Seacoast has been able to grow larger and smaller at the same time without losing its distinct identity.

What about You?

Established larger churches like Southeast Christian and Prestonwood feel it is important to reproduce the original campus as closely as possible, while churches like Seacoast see an advantage in "right-sizing" campuses to fit a community or culture. But what size campus best fits the vision of *your* church? Take time to consider your unique identity as a church. Do you need to replicate all the ministries and advantages of a large original site, or do you see niche opportunities to impact a unique community or culture? How can you best leverage the resources God has given you?

Your questions may be more about strategy than about size or location: How does launching a new campus differ from planting a new church? Could starting an off-site campus be a way to jump-start planting an independent church? To find the answers to these questions, we head to New Hope Christian Fellowship in Honolulu, Hawaii. Grab your flip-flops and some sunscreen. Surf's up!

2 THE CHURCH PLANTING VERSUS CAMPUS LAUNCH DILEMMA

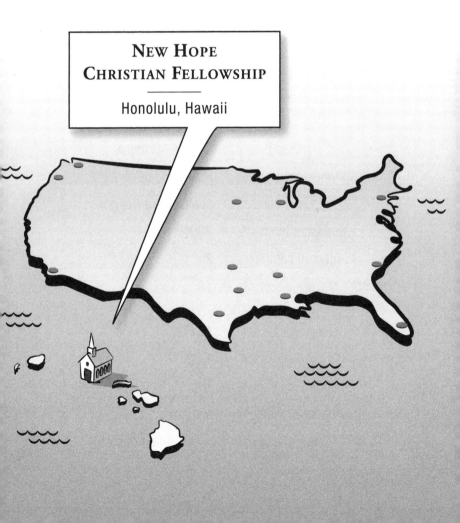

NEW HOPE
CHRISTIAN FELLOWSHIP

Honolulu, Hawaii

NEW HOPE CHRISTIAN FELLOWSHIP

FAST FACTS

Church vision ▶ *To present the gospel of Jesus Christ in such a way that turns non-Christians into converts, converts into disciples, and disciples into mature, fruitful leaders who will in turn go into the world and reach others for Christ.*

Year founded ▶ *1995*

Original location ▶ *Honolulu, Hawaii*

Lead pastor ▶ *Wayne Cordeiro*

Teaching model for off-sites ▶ *Primarily video/DVD*

Denomination ▶ *Foursquare Gospel*

Year went multi-site ▶ *2001*

Number of campuses ▶ *7*

Number of weekly services ▶ *18*

Worship attendance (all physical sites) ▶ *11,000*

Largest room's seating capacity ▶ *1,200*

Internet campus? ▶ *Yes*

International campus? ▶ *No*

Internet address ▶ *www.enewhope.org*

When a new idea emerges, there are always those who will simply grab it and run with it. Many of those who do church planting have now widely embraced the multi-site idea. It's hard to go to a conference anywhere on starting new churches without hearing serious buzz about using multi-site as a church-planting strategy.

I (Warren) remember my first visit, back in 2001, to New Hope Christian Fellowship in Honolulu, where Wayne Cordeiro is lead pastor. The church was bursting at the seams. Going early to the public high school they were renting, I watched volunteer setup teams do an amazing transformation of the campus. They converted classrooms into rooms suitable for children's ministry. They unpacked tents to be used for greeting newcomers or helping people join a ministry. They set up video cameras and an elaborate sound system. They even cleaned the school's bathrooms. They used almost every square inch of the campus for two Saturday evening services and four Sunday morning services.

Yet people from New Hope were still inviting family and friends, who in turn invited their family and friends. Where would the church put all these people? Purchasing a suitable location in Honolulu was out of the question: no large land tracts were available, and the multi-million-dollar price per acre was prohibitive. Would the church soon reach capacity and need to put out a No Vacancy sign?

Wayne's approach has always been to make more room, and to do it by training more leaders. He has built into them a dream, not just to develop New Hope Honolulu but also to plant like-minded churches around the world. Several of those churches were started on the island of Oahu, with people who were driving to New Hope Honolulu from neighboring towns. Many of these same people have now become the core groups for satellite campuses of New Hope.

We had the chance to experience one of these campuses: New Hope Leeward, led by Mike Lwin. Geoff had the difficult assignment of visiting them on-site in Hawaii, and I later conducted a follow-up interview by phone.

Avoiding Spam in Hawaii

Sometimes in ministry you have to make tough decisions; deciding whether or not I (Geoff) should accept Pastor Mike Lwin's invitation to visit him at New Hope in Honolulu was *not* one of those. One of my core values is that I always say yes when someone invites me to come to Hawaii. Free trips to Italy and Bali fall in the same category in my decision-making matrix.

I learned several important things in Hawaii, not the least of which is that Spam, introduced to the Islands during World War II by American GIs, is considered a delicacy by the natives. Available at fine dining establishments like McDonald's and Burger King, Spam is known as "the Hawaiian steak." Having been forced to dine on Spam as a child, I chose to pass on the opportunity to reacquaint myself with Hormel's exotic cuisine.

While I avoided the various flavors of Spam in Hawaii, I did not pass on the different flavors of multi-site at New Hope and enjoyed getting a taste of the distinct New Hope culture that unifies all their campuses and church plants.

Our exposure to New Hope culture started as soon as we arrived in Hawaii. When we landed in Honolulu (I say "we" because my wife and daughter had volunteered to accompany me on this trip in case a beach crisis arose during my stay), Mike and his son greeted our late-night flight with flower leis and warm Hawaiian greetings. Throughout our stay we found that this "aloha spirit" is a core value for New Hope Church. At every meeting and service we attended, we were welcomed into New Hope's *ohana*, or family.

On Sunday we toured three of the New Hope sites. At New Hope Diamond Head we met a man who comes every morning at four thirty to cook breakfast for the "Levites" (volunteers) who arrive at six o'clock to set up church in a quaint community playhouse that New Hope rents on weekends. The cook insisted that we sample the saimin, an Asian-style noodle dish. At New Hope Windward, which meets at the Regal Theater, my daughter loved the Frito pie offered to everyone who attends. Last but not least, we arrived at New Hope Leeward and were treated to homemade pineapple cake and fruit salad, rounding out our Sunday morning progressive meal.

New Hope's culture exhibits great hospitality in everything they do. They clearly embrace a passion for evangelism, for relationally based leadership development, for doing church as a team, for being gracious in all their dealings, for growth in devotion to God's Word, and for personal spiritual maturity, in a way that causes people to put gentleness and care into all their actions.[5]

Yet that New Hope DNA is not exclusive to their satellite campuses or Hawaiian church plants. Wayne Cordeiro's vision is to impact the entire Pacific Rim with life-giving churches. More than fifty students and graduates from New Hope–sponsored Pacific Rim Bible College have served on church-plant teams in Hawaii and the Pacific Rim.

From Campus to Church Plant

New Hope Leeward is an excellent example of how New Hope's satellite breakouts represent their church-planting plan. "Our goal for satellites is not necessarily to add locations," explains Wayne. "It is to develop new leaders. It is to edge these emerging leaders into their own teaching, where one day we can release them as stand-alone churches. When young leaders go out with this model, they have time to build relationships, develop teams, think about evangelism projects, do community outreach, and build leaders," he says.[6]

When Mike launched New Hope Leeward under Wayne, the site followed a video download approach for most of its weekly teaching. Everything was centralized, including the finances. Mike focused his time and energy on developing leaders. Gradually, as Mike showed increased success in the ministry, Wayne began to release different areas of responsibility to him, including much of the teaching. Over a three-year period, the satellite became an independently registered Foursquare denomination church, following in the footsteps of its parent.

During this phase of growth, the new Leeward church launched two of its own satellite campuses. While these satellites may eventually become independent churches, there is no plan for them to do so at present. Weekly worship attendance at Leeward and the two satellite campuses averages about twenty-five hundred.

While New Hope Leeward and New Hope Honolulu model the same overall DNA, there are also small but important variations. Mike and his team are mostly in their thirties, so the church activities reach a younger demographic than those of New Hope Honolulu. Likewise, the children's programs offer slightly different emphases in what they teach. To Mike and his teammates, this flexibility is part of the benefit that comes with being a church plant rather than a satellite campus.

Some New Hope campuses will likely remain satellites, while others are in the process of becoming independent churches. Each local campus pastor makes the decision in conjunction with Wayne, enabling each campus to follow a model that fits its leadership and leads to maximum growth potential. "Some leaders thrive under strong corporate structure, some do better independent, others do best somewhere in between," says Mike McGuire, multi-site Executive Pastor of New Hope Leeward.

Church Planting as Later Development

While New Hope in Hawaii exemplifies an *intentional* plan for developing satellite campuses into independent congregations, other churches are *unintentionally* moving in that same direction. Many of the older, denominational "first churches" located in urban settings throughout the United States have been embracing the multi-site model as an alternative to leaving the city. Instead of selling the downtown facility because their members have moved to the suburbs, the church will often retain the urban campus and, for a while, enjoy the best of both worlds by starting a second campus in the suburbs. Over time, however, the pastoral staff changes, the congregations develop distinct identities, fewer joint ventures are conducted, and eventually the dual-campus plan turns into a church plant as the second congregation becomes a separate church.

Church Planting and Satellite Campuses Together

A third model for church planting involves developing two parallel tracks—both planting independent churches and starting new campuses. Saddleback Church, where Rick Warren is pastor, has planted several dozen churches across Southern California. In 2006 Saddleback also went multi-site, and they have plans to develop ten campuses across Orange County by 2010 while also continuing to plant new churches.

Other churches have developed entire organizations to support this two-track approach. In 2001 Seacoast (profiled in the last chapter) was a founding member of the Association of Related Churches, an organization designed to help foster church planting. Community Christian Church (profiled in chapter 8), in Naperville, Illinois, has nine campuses and has created the New Thing Network, an organization that serves as a catalyst for developing a movement of reproducing churches. Leaders who are part of the New Thing Network can travel on either track, becoming part of a multi-site campus or helping launch an affiliated, independent congregation.

Deciding Whether to Plant a Church or Launch a Campus

Many churches ask about the difference between creating a new campus and planting a totally separate new church. The idea of one church in multiple locations typically means that you share a common vision, budget, leadership, and board. If your new campus has a vision, budget, leader, or board that's not part of the sending campus, you've planted a new church or mission campus, not a multi-site campus.

Why do some churches choose to become multi-site rather than spin off new churches? The advantages of being multi-site include greater accountability, sharing of resources (stewardship), the infusion of trained workers, shared DNA (vision and core values), greater prayer support, a preestablished network for problem solving, not needing to reinvent the wheel, and connection with others doing the same thing.

So how do you decide whether to plant a church or launch a campus? You might prayerfully work through questions like these:

▶ *Is church planting or campus addition more a part of the DNA of our church?* People and churches most readily reproduce what they are and know already.

▶ *What is the gifting and passion of the leader you are considering?* Campus pastors come alongside the vision of the directional leader (the person who heads the team, casts the vision, and leads the church's forward movement) and help develop that vision in their location; church planters have the vision (and the calling) to plant a church.

▶ *What is the proximity of the new entity to an existing campus of your church?* If within a short commute, it's better to form a campus rather than a new church, to minimize any sense of competition for resources.

▶ *What level of resource investment is desired?* Church plants can require less of a financial investment, whereas in most cases campuses are a larger investment.

Many churches can avoid a lot of hurt feelings down the road by deciding in advance if the location will be a plant or a campus and then making that expectation clear to the local leadership involved.

Looking Ahead

Whatever you do, you'll need to choose the extent to which you will be embracing the multi-site concept. If you decide to go multi-site, will your church be one church *with* additional campuses or one church *of* multiple campuses? To understand this crucial distinction, we'll be heading off to the hilly landscape of Little Rock, Arkansas.

FELLOWSHIP BIBLE CHURCH

Little Rock, Arkansas

FELLOWSHIP BIBLE CHURCH

FAST FACTS

Church vision ▸ **To equip and unleash Christ followers to change the world through lives of irresistible influence.**

Year founded ▸ **1977**

Original location ▸ **Little Rock, Arkansas**

Lead pastor ▸ **Tim Lundy**

Teaching model for off-sites ▸ **Primarily video/DVD**

Denomination ▸ **Nondenominational**

Year went multi-site ▸ **2003**

Number of campuses ▸ **3**

Number of weekly services ▸ **10**

Worship attendance (all physical sites) ▸ **6,300**

Largest room's seating capacity ▸ **1,500**

Internet campus? ▸ **No**

International campus? ▸ **No**

Internet address ▸ **www.fellowshiponline.com**

A multi-site church is either a church with multiple sites or a church of multiple sites. Making the all-important shift from with to of brings a significant change to the culture of the church. This subtle shift transforms the core identity of the church and will affect everything you do.

For our next stop, we pay a visit to Little Rock, Arkansas, to experience the story of Fellowship Bible Church — a congregation that made the journey from a church *with* to a church *of*, a shift that happened in the midst of relocating their original campus.

I (Greg) first met Tim Lundy, pastor and directional leader at Fellowship Bible Church, back in early 2003. It was my first time in Little Rock, and I had come because I wanted to get a taste of the three venues they had recently set up on their campus. In addition to their main sanctuary, where they had been meeting for Sunday morning services for several years, the church had now expanded their worship to the chapel and the gym.

When I got out of my car, I immediately wished I had worn my New Balance running shoes rather than my Allen Edmond dress shoes. That particular section of Little Rock is quite hilly. I could see that this church facility wouldn't follow a typical layout, with a central entrance, sanctuary to the left, chapel to the right, and gym down the hall! Instead their campus was a collection of different buildings on multiple levels, with parking and walkways connecting it all.

Fellowship Bible had expanded its worship to three locations to relieve the pressure that rapid growth had created on its seating capacity. With a full auditorium, they had already been holding two services every weekend. So they'd put a lot of prayer, thought, and conversation into the process of transitioning to other locations on their campus.

During my visit, I was eager to visit all three venues: the original venue, carried by a contemporary, seeker-oriented style of worship; *The Edge* venue, located in the gym of the church's student ministry facility; and *The Chapel* venue, located in the chapel and characterized by a more unplugged style of worship and ministry.

Having had only one cup of coffee that morning and finding myself in need of a wake-up call, I decided to make my first visit to *The Edge* venue. Like each of the venues, it featured live music—in this case hard-driving rock and roll, perfect to get my eyes open and blood flowing! The worship set was followed by a welcome from the campus pastor and a lead-in to Tim's video teaching segment, recorded from an earlier service.

The service bulletin cued me in to the direction and length of the message, so at about the middle of teaching point number two, I slid out the back door and headed over the hill and through the woods (just kidding on the woods part) to the original auditorium, to hear the conclusion of Tim's live message. The service in that venue concluded with a post-teaching set of praise-team-led contemporary Christian worship.

After the first service, I grabbed my fourth cup of joe for the day and headed to *The Chapel*—not to get married (happily married for ten years at the time) but to experience Fellowship Bible Church's third venue. I was warmly greeted and ushered into "the church I grew up in": rows of seats facing a pulpit, with an illuminated cross on the back wall. The lights were low, and the live acoustic music was pleasant to the ear. I joined in singing some hymns and then enjoyed the first half of Tim's sermon once again, also by video. It's amazing what you can learn when you are really awake!

On my way out to meet Tim and his team for lunch, I got the sense that the launch of the two new venues was going well and was helping the church to free up additional seats in the central auditorium. Though my visit was mainly to observe the different venues and interview Tim and his team about their multi-site model, our lunch conversation quickly moved to other issues facing the church as it entered its annual strategic planning season.

We talked about small groups and missions, leadership development, children's ministry, and even Tim's changing role as he assumed more of the directional leader role from the previous lead pastor, Robert Lewis. It was clear that the venues were only one piece (and a small one at that) of a much bigger picture for Tim and the team. Although the venues were an important part of the church's strategy, they were only one programmatic aspect of Fellowship Bible Church's plan to reach more people for Christ in the Greater Little Rock area. They were useful but not essential to the church's identity.

From "With" to "Of"

Let's fast-forward eight months to November 2003 and Leadership Network's Multi-Site Churches Leadership Community, a gathering of a dozen churches committed to developing a multi-site approach. Shortly after my initial visit with his team, Tim had come to the first meeting of the Leadership Community. By this time, Tim and his team had completed their annual strategic planning regimen and had an entire year of doing ministry in multiple venues under their belt.

Tim shared with the group his team's observation that during their strategic planning meetings, the multiple venues kept coming up in every conversation. He and his team were finding that the multi-site strategy was having an impact everywhere. When they began to discuss the future direction for children's ministry, everyone recognized the huge possibilities available by tailoring them to the various venues. When they addressed the age-old challenge of discovering and developing leaders in a large, growing church, the conversation went to new places as they considered the opportunities with multiple venues.

> The expansion to multiple venues was no longer an isolated strategy — it was affecting everything the church did.

Venues weren't driving everything in the church (nor should they), but they were inevitably a part of every discussion. The expansion to multiple venues was no longer an isolated strategy — it was affecting everything the church did.

As the Fellowship Bible team shared their findings at the Leadership Community, they met others who had pioneered the multi-site vision. They listened as LifeChurch.tv (profiled in chapters 6 and 10) shared their discovery that they weren't structured for their vision, and learned how LifeChurch.tv had "blown up" their organization chart to strategically align their leadership with their reality of multi-site ministry. Tim and his teammates were impressed with Community Christian's reproducing-campus model (see chapter 8) and Christ the King's organic approach (see chapter 9). Gathering together the insights from that meeting, Tim came to an astute conclusion: "We have a decision to make — we will either be a church *with* multiple venues or a church *of* multiple venues."

> "We have a decision to make — we will either be a church *with* multiple venues or a church *of* multiple venues."

The change from *with* to *of* is subtle, but it transforms everything you do as a multi-site church. You can no longer discuss student ministry or men's ministry or pastoral care or you-fill-in-the-blank ministry without recognizing the implications for each venue or campus. When you decide to be a church *of* multiple venues or campuses, multi-site becomes a foundational underpinning for all the strategies of the church. It involves a significant change in philosophy and a commitment to making the changes necessary for effective execution. Once Fellowship Bible Church recognized the need, they made the strategic decision to shift their identity and began the process of transition to a church *of* multiple venues.

Transition Issues — Replication and Community

Recently I asked Tim to reflect on a couple of the transitions that took place as Fellowship Bible became a church *of* multiple venues (on-site)

DNA IS ON YOUR SIDE

Your church's DNA is your core identity—it's what attracts others to your church. Tom Cheyney, author of numerous books on church planting, notes, "The same can be said of a multi-site or multi-campus church. My father's generation would select a church because it was of a particular denomination. We were loyal to that denomination. When our family moved into a new area, we would seek that particular type of congregational affiliation out. That is no longer the case. Today, the loyalty is towards a style and a particular DNA. Gone are the days of strong ties to any particular denominational precept. That is not good or bad news; it is just a fact that pastors today must realize." It is important to have your church's DNA on your side, working for you.

Tom Cheyney, "The Multi-Site Church Planting
Strategy: Possibly the Most Effective Channel
for 'Doing Church' in the 21st Century!"

www.ChurchPlantingVillage.net.

and campuses (different locations). He explained that the change really began when they focused their attention on replicating their children's ministry. While Fellowship Bible Church was known in the community for their phenomenal children's ministry, the excellence of its children's programming was staff intensive and facility dependent. Tim said, "When we tried to export it from our same-campus venues to other campuses, it just didn't work. It was too dependent on physical space and paid staff." Recognizing this led them to initiate some conversations about simplifying the ministry for multiplication. Tim described this to me as a season of integration. His team began the process by asking the question, "Can what we do be replicated?"

> His team began the process by asking the question, "Can what we do be replicated?"

The centralized, original campus staff took a second look at their existing ministries. They began to ask different questions: Do we need this huge machine to make it happen? How do we take this ministry and develop it in such a way that other campuses can pull it off? These questions led to some key changes and gave birth to a reproducible model of ministry.

In his 2008 address at Catalyst in Atlanta, Georgia, Jim Collins of *Good to Great* fame highlighted some key issues that impact replication of DNA—the genes that shape every cell of an organism. He noted that great organizations (and in our case great churches) have a culture of discipline demonstrated by a history of making choices that lead to that greatness. "Most overnight successes are really about twenty years in the making," he said. "It took seven years for Sam Walton to open his second store. It took Starbucks thirteen years before they had five stores." Once greatness is achieved, the DNA is set and replication can effectively begin. The same is true, we believe, for multi-site churches. In these churches, we find that the core DNA of the congregation has been developed over time. Time-tested core vision, mission, and values must be present in each venue or campus. In fact, a clear and widely shared DNA becomes the engine for expansion—but it must be reproducible.

> A clear and widely shared DNA becomes the engine for expansion—but it must be reproducible.

The second transition occurred when Fellowship Bible Church learned to trust that moving to multiple venues didn't mean they had to sacrifice authentic community. One of the main barriers to multi-site expansion is the irrational belief that people are in community because they show up at the same physical space each week. As Tim cast vision for multiple venues and later multiple campuses, he helped people see that authentic connections and real community are found with the people they worship with each week.

The truth is that there are thousands of other people attending a different worship service each week whom they do not know. Even in the same service, people sit far apart and might never meet each other. Tim helped people understand that the transition to on-site venues and eventually to additional campuses would actually offer them greater opportunities for connection through smaller groupings of people. The close bonds with families and friends that they shared each week in community worship were now available in the venue of their choice.

> One of the main barriers to multi-site expansion is the irrational belief that people are in community because they show up at the same physical space each week.

Looking beyond the limitations of their physical space, the staff at the church helped people understand that it's the other parts of church life that connect them in community—not the building. Having taken the people through this transition, Tim believes, "We are more connected as a church than ever before."

Setting the New DNA in Concrete

In October 2005 the opportunity came for Fellowship Bible Church to put its money where its leadership's mouth was. Tim and the elders were approached by the school adjacent to their campus with an offer to purchase most of the church's property.

Years earlier the church had the foresight to buy a tract of land in an area of Little Rock where they anticipated growth. The long-term expectation was that they would relocate the church, building a larger campus to house both the existing ministries and the anticipated growth. But all these plans had been made prior to their discovery of multi-site options.

As conversations with the school continued, the next phase of the vision began to unfold. In April 2006 Tim and the elders unveiled a plan to "downsize for growth." Though the team didn't actually place a For Sale sign on the church lawn, the sale of the church's twenty-five-acre campus embodied their commitment to multi-site as an ongoing part of its future.

Most of the existing, original campus was sold to the school, and the administrative building to another organization, and a design for a new, smaller church facility on the west Little Rock property was developed.

The new campus opened on May 18, 2008, and Tim reports that it has been a night-and-day difference. The two-hundred-thousand-square-foot facility was built entirely under one roof. As the building design was being developed, Tim had some keen insight into what would support Fellowship Bible Church's multi-site DNA. "We knew that anything we built had to be in synch with our values as a church, and once again, one of the central values is authentic community. This led us to design a space that was welcoming, intimate, and centered around space for community gatherings and connection."

While the new worship center is still the largest venue, the number of seats was reduced from that of the original campus's auditorium. But seating in the other two venues was increased to accommodate growth. A warehouse space, which houses *The Edge* venue, can seat 800, and *The Chapel* venue seats 550. The end result is a more intimate experience in all three venues.

As an extension of their value for community, Fellowship Bible wanted every door of their facility to feel like a front door. So the new building has four entrances, with parking completely encircling it. No matter which entrance you use, you are led into the community concourse—an area at the center of all the activity. The venues are in three of the corners, and the children's building and student ministry round out the facility. Everything feeds into the community gathering space, creating great opportunities for connection and providing the congregation with a regular, visual, experiential reminder that they are one church.

Two fascinating things have happened since the opening of this new building. First, some of the pioneering members of Fellowship Bible have communicated to Tim, "We've been here for twenty-five years, and this feels like the old church again. This feels like the early days." Second, as people have experienced community in multiple venues, they have begun to understand the vision for additional campuses.

Tim said that even those who originally were the most vocally opposed to the idea have begun to embrace the other venues. The experience of authentic community in multiple venues has led many to believe that they could realize this connection with other sites as well. The congregation has come to recognize that transitioning to multi-site doesn't necessarily mean sacrificing a community feel. If anything, the multi-site model can actually deepen the community experience.

Impact on Leadership Structure

Moving from a church *with* to a church *of* multiple sites also necessitated a change in leadership structure. Fellowship Bible Church had historically been led by a management team composed of three teaching pastors. The "*of* multiple locations" DNA required an expanded team. As Tim said, "We realized we needed leadership outside of what a teaching pastor can bring. This approach to church requires some different skill sets, and so we put an executive team in place."

This new executive team includes the teaching pastors as well as other executive staff pastors who provide leadership for the church's equipping and unleashing ministries, and central services that support those ministries. In addition, a former campus pastor has a seat on the executive team. Tim indicated that this addition is crucial because you need someone who has lived on a campus full-time to help the team ask questions about the impact of corporate decisions on individual campuses.

Leadership DNA through the Worship Team

For a number of years, multi-site churches have recognized that one of the keys for a successful venue or campus launch is having the right leadership in place. Most of the conversations have focused on the strategic leadership of the campus or venue pastor. And while the role of these pastors is emphasized at Fellowship Bible, Tim and his team are discovering that another leadership role is key in extending the church DNA into each venue and campus. It's the role of the worship leader.

At their old campus, venues were led in worship by teams that rotated between them, changing the worship styles but maintaining centralized leadership. At the new campuses, as people are developing deeper relationships and showing a strong affinity for their particular venue, they are also responding to the worship changes that accompanied the move. The transition to multiple campuses ushered in a new worship model with dedicated teams in each venue. For Fellowship Bible, the consistency in up-front leadership of the worship team in each venue created just as much stability as did that of the venue pastor. With the combination of a dedicated pastor and a consistent worship team, the people gathered in each venue have begun to develop a sense of ownership and have deepened in their relationships with one another. The DNA of Fellowship Bible is still guided by the common thread of collaboration that happens among the worship teams, but the freedom afforded the individual teams allows for the creation of a unique experience in each venue.

Signs That the DNA Is Embedded

How will Fellowship Bible know that they have arrived? How will they know that they have made the transition from a church *with* to a church *of*? Tim is quick to say that you don't ever completely get there. There will always be a need to recast vision and demonstrate the value and impact of the model. However, there are some leading indicators that show they are well on their way to reshaping the core identity of the church.

▶ *Multi-site assumed.* The first sign of an embedded multi-site DNA at Fellowship Bible is that multi-site is not an issue of contention. Tim and his team are no longer expending valuable energy convincing people of its value. Quite the contrary. Tim said, "I realized one day that it has become something assumed." The leadership and staff are designed to lead according to this model. The body is finding connection to their venue or campus, and those with an evangelistic heart or entrepreneurial spirit are asking, "When is the next launch? Sign me up!"

▶ *Multi-site thinking.* Tim noted, "As our executive team has expanded, we have added leaders who have joined us with the multi-site DNA already embedded. They did not have to make the transition. They didn't have to learn how to think differently. From day one they were thinking multi-site. Key leadership living and breathing multi-site is a key sign and key sustainer of the 'church *of* multiple venues and campuses' DNA."

▶ *Multi-site fruit.* As they say, the proof is in the pudding—or more biblically, "by their fruit you will recognize them" (Matt. 7:16). The results of the model at Fellowship Bible demonstrate that each of the venues and campuses are really serving as front doors to the larger, unified church. And more doors mean more opportunities for people to walk through and meet Jesus.

Tim shared with me recently a story about a family who had been impacted in a powerful way as a result of their connection with one of Fellowship Bible Church's campuses. Sue and her kids were victims of domestic violence. The south campus of the church joined in a Habitat for Humanity project to build her a house. As they built her home, they also built a relationship with her. Sue and her kids connected with Jesus Christ through them, and now she and her two teenage sons attend the south campus.

DNA Comes with Any Age

The story of Fellowship Bible in Little Rock, Arkansas, is not unique. The DNA for multi-site can be embedded into a church of any age or denomination. Three hundred miles north of Little Rock, Pastor Jim Downing asked members of First United Methodist Church of

Sedalia, Missouri—a long-established rural congregation—to open their wallets and purses and take out pictures of their children and grandchildren. The people happily showed the photos to each other.

"Does everyone in these pictures go to church? Do they all have an active faith in Jesus Christ?" the pastor probed.

The mood in the room changed. Many shook their heads.

"What would you do," he continued, "if a church in the town where *they* lived would reach out to them and provide a place for them to say yes to life, to love, and to God?"

The congregation overwhelmingly agreed, "We'd do almost anything to see that happen."

The pastor now had both their interest and their hearts. "I believe there are Christians in other cities whose children or grandchildren have moved to *this* area, who are praying for a church here in Sedalia to do the same thing—to reach out to them. *What if God is calling us to be that church?*"

So began the decision of an old but growing congregation, with its facility one block off the county courthouse square, to add a second campus 2.7 miles away. There are only thirty thousand people in the entire county, but the church caught a vision for their seventeen thousand friends and neighbors who do not attend any church. With a say-yes attitude, the congregation was determined to create a new campus with the understanding that it was for someone else.

From those 1997 discussions, when annual attendance averaged 136 for the year, it was a bold step for the congregation to open a new campus in 1999. Today, combining both sites, more than 814 people worship with First Church. Almost 325 of the newest people have come to faith in Jesus Christ since joining First Church. And weekly there are more than 450 people serving in a ministry that fits them.

Where Does Your Church Stand?

How about your church? Is God calling you to make the shift from *with* to *of*? If so, you will need to do the hard work of clarifying your core identity. Your DNA—vision, mission, and values—must be owned and honed as you move forward toward God's vision for your church and community. Costly work? Yes. But consider the potential for impact on your community. The value? Priceless!

As we continue our roadtrip, let's load up and head south to San Antonio, Texas, for a lesson in real estate. We'll take a look at the variety of locations where multi-site campuses are being developed—sometimes in places you wouldn't expect!

4 YOU WANT TO LAUNCH A CAMPUS *WHERE?*

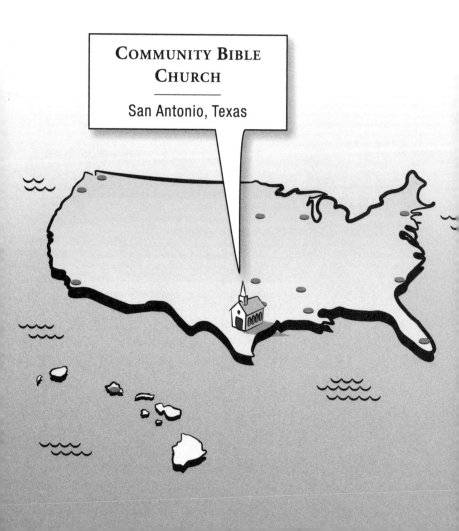

COMMUNITY BIBLE CHURCH

San Antonio, Texas

COMMUNITY BIBLE CHURCH

FAST FACTS

Church vision ▶ *To reach, teach, and help people in Jesus' name through large group celebrations, small group ministries, and lots of locations.*

Year founded ▶ *1990*

Original location ▶ *San Antonio, Texas*

Lead pastor ▶ *Robert Emmitt*

Teaching model for off-sites ▶ *Combination video/DVD and campus pastors teaching in person*

Denomination ▶ *Nondenominational*

Year went multi-site ▶ *2006*

Number of campuses ▶ *9*

Number of weekly services ▶ *14*

Worship attendance (all physical sites) ▶ *13,000*

Largest room's seating capacity ▶ *3,500*

Internet campus? ▶ *No*

International campus? ▶ *Yes*

Internet address ▶ *www.communitybible.com*

Choosing the right location for the next campus is one of the most difficult decisions for a multi-site church. Each church's vision, values, and context help it shape the strategy that will have the greatest kingdom impact.

Churches open additional campuses in a variety of locations to address immediate needs for space as well as longer-term opportunities to connect with more diverse audiences, engage in strategic partnerships, and create local ownership. Our time spent deep in the heart of Texas (San Antonio) with Community Bible Church will assist us in answering several questions: What makes for a good location? How do you choose the right location for establishing a new site? What factors need to be considered?

My (Greg's) dad spent twenty-five years in the franchise business as a McDonald's owner-operator in the panhandle of Texas. I remember conversations we had as I was growing up, when I asked him about the success of his restaurants. Along with needing to invest 483 hours of hard work each week (I know there are only 168 hours in a week, but you'd agree with me if you knew my dad!), he always said that one essential key to success is *location*. I've been to a lot of McDonald's stores over the years, noting their consistently well-placed locations. My wife and I have also purchased and sold several homes along the way, and the real-estate mantra of "location, location, location" still rings in my ears.

For Robert Emmitt and Community Bible Church, location is a key factor in multi-site ministry success. But as with a McDonald's site, prime location alone is not enough; there are many wonderfully situated church facilities that people pass by without a second thought. In addition to a good location, you need inviting "food" — and some highly regarded people too! As I would learn through my visit,

Community Bible is a leader in finding unique ways to do ministry—"food" and people—in a variety of locations.

I first met Robert in May 2006 at the Multi-Site Coast to Coast conference in Charleston, South Carolina. He and several people on his team were on an exploratory trip to look at Seacoast Church and the two other churches—North Coast and Community Christian—that shared the platform at that conference. I remember Robert asking me in his straight-shooting but humble manner if I thought this multi-site deal was real. I told him why I was convinced. After he and his team spent time with the pioneering churches onstage at the conference, they went home believing that it was at least worth a try.

And try they did. One of the things from the multi-site conference that stood out for Robert was the statement that adding one additional campus was pretty easy, adding two was an efficient strategy, adding three bumped up the stress load for your team, and adding four just plumb wore your people out. So he and his team decided to take a big step of faith and start at least *ten* new campuses!

The Community Bible Church Story

Community Bible Church hit the ground running, launching two campuses just months after the decision to go multi-site. These two sites were started at roughly the same time, both using proven church staff as campus pastors. The first campus currently meets in a rehabbed retail location in northwest San Antonio. On a phone-call update with Robert, he indicated that its pastor "had been on staff with us for years, heading up our life groups and doing a variety of leadership and ministry training. He was an excellent pastor, so we built that around his leadership." The second campus in Bulverde, north of San Antonio, was launched by the Community Bible pastor of small groups. "He was one of those rare people they write about in books, the kind who can start a group, grow it, multiply leaders, and spin off new groups—someone who actually multiplied groups well," Robert said. That campus meets in a public school. According to Leadership Network surveys, schools are the most popular places for churches to rent, whether for multi-site campuses or new church plants.

Community Bible continued to grow and multiply new campuses. After launching the first two in 2006, they followed with three more within the next year. And they weren't afraid to learn from new ideas! I had the chance to visit Robert and his team at Community Bible while visiting other churches in the San Antonio area, and I asked them if they had ever worked with the YMCA. I shared with them the amazing story of Stillwater United Methodist Church in Dayton, Ohio, a church profiled in our first book, *The Multi-Site Church Revolution*.[7] Stillwater had forged an innovative partnership with a local YMCA, utilizing their space for a new campus and sharing the costs with the organization. For a very small financial investment that covered the costs of upgrading the wiring and acoustics so the gym would be a suitable place for worship, Stillwater was able to establish a new campus that served another portion of the city. Robert asked a few probing questions, and the wheels began to turn.

The next thing I knew, I received an email from Robert announcing the launch of their campus in Boerne (a far northwest suburb) — in a newly constructed YMCA! Several months later they followed up with the launch of their campus in New Braunfels (a far northeast suburb) — also in a YMCA. Grass does not grow under Robert Emmitt's feet! In his own words, the launch of new campuses is motivated by an overwhelming sense of need: "The need is great, and the opportunities for sharing the gospel through multiple campuses are increasing. I would love to launch one hundred campuses over the next ten years!"

By early 2009 Community Bible Church was involved in ministry on nine campuses, including an international campus in Lake Chapala, Mexico (see chapter 9, which deals specifically with international campuses). The eight off-site campuses represent about 12 percent of total attendance (1,300 of 11,000), with average attendance of about 150 people each. Every campus is financially self-supporting, regardless of size — whether they are 80 or 300.

Location Realities:
What Works and What Doesn't

Very few multi-site churches take McDonald's original approach to design, in which all facilities are almost a clone of the original (McDonald's would describe this as an intentional part of their brand). Community Bible's original campus, for example, is highly visible and easily accessible from an interstate-quality highway. It was built as a church facility in a growing section of town, and those driving by would easily guess that a church meets in that location.

But none of Community Bible's off-site congregations meet in facilities anything like the original campus. Community Bible has campuses in a shopping center (which it leased long-term and remodeled), YMCA facilities, an event center, and various local schools (elementary school, middle school, and high school).

With so many diverse locations to choose from, how do churches like Community Bible decide where to plant a campus? What criteria should churches use when evaluating potential sites? Based on our visits to Community Bible's campuses and to a combined three-author total of over one hundred different multi-site locations, plus various interviews and surveys we've conducted, we'd like to suggest seven key factors that should be assessed when choosing a location:

1. *Positive community image.* What is the perception of the location in the community? If there are negative associations with the location, is it a place that could be transformed into a positive asset for the community? Can a dead location be brought back to life? One church recently attempted to launch a campus in what seemed to be an ideal location: the rent was cheap, and there was a fully equipped chapel, ample rooms for children's ministry, and plenty of parking. Unfortunately, the campus failed when they discovered that the community wasn't dying to attend church in a funeral parlor! (A few churches, however, have figured out how to work the funeral chapel location to their advantage, but they're the exception.)

2. *Location accessibility.* Is the location near the people you want to reach? Can they get to it easily, by car or public transportation? Seacoast has a campus in what seems to be an ideal location. The building is right off a major freeway near a growing area of town. Unfortunately, to find the building, you need a compass, a guide dog, and a GPS. Several staff members have gotten lost trying to find the campus (we're still looking for some of them).

3. *Facility accessibility.* How accessible is the facility? Can moms with strollers, or older people with hip issues, enter without problems? In our previous book, we shared the comical story of Seacoast's short-lived experiment in renting an arena. The facility had plenty of parking spots, but visitors had to travel through a mile-long maze of narrow corridors to get to the right place.

4. *Room for growth.* Once you're settled in at a location, you probably don't want to move again right away. Can you make the location inviting and comfortable as you anticipate future growth? How would it look at different stages of growth—if you should double or triple in size? I (Warren) was part of a church that moved six times in six months. The pastor greeted everyone weekly with a smile and the statement, "People get to come to this church only if they can find us, and we're glad you're part of that special group this week!" Unfortunately, the "special group" gradually got smaller and smaller because the community came to see the church as an unstable fly-by-night operation.

5. *Noise tolerance.* Can the location accommodate loud music, laughter, and even loud preaching? In quiet moments, can it foster adequate reflection? These are not a given for most portable churches—the ones that set up weekly in schools and part-time locations. I (Warren) attended a multi-site church that always rented the banquet room of a hotel. Everything was great—except for the Asian airline group that rented the room next to us once a month. For employee

awards, they would use a large gong that made an unnaturally loud crashing sound with a long reverberation. Apparently, lots of their employees were winning awards, because the gong went off continually at unexpected times!

6. *Decent rent or purchase price.* It seems as if every multi-site church has a wonderful story of God at work giving them a great price on a rental location or on a facility for sale. However, if a deal seems too good to be true, that may be the case. One Connecticut church preparing to go multi-site bought a property at a fantastic price, only to find out that its entire perimeter was a designated wetland, protected by law. They weren't even able to get onto their own property! Their case is currently in court. Be cautious when you find a great deal.

7. *Room for storage.* This is one of the biggest issues for portable multi-site churches. I (Greg) remember one of my first visits to Willow Creek's North Shore Campus. When I received the tour of the private school that housed it, I remember being shown "the storage room." You would have thought I was being ushered into the Holy of Holies. My guide thoughtfully pointed out how the very small space had been maximized to pack in lots of equipment and supplies.

Another church in Louisiana solved their storage challenges through a unique partnership with a public school. The school had long-term plans to build a workout facility for their student athletes. The church agreed to provide the capital needed to build the external storage structure for that facility. This decision brought the school a step closer to providing new space for their athletic program and created a storage space adjacent to the school's auditorium, where worship services were held each weekend.

Entire industries have sprung up to help churches pack all their stuff in rolling carts and tightly packed trailers. It rarely hurts to have a lockable, safe storage area for a church's more fragile items, such as sound boards or speakers, so you don't have to transport them outside in the elements weekly. Sometimes, however, it's hard to know what is safe. Seacoast's Asheville campus pastor arrived early one Sunday at the theater where his congregation met. Behind the theater, he discovered that a car had smashed into their storage container during the night. Several pieces of equipment were destroyed, and the entire container had to be replaced. Thankfully, the perpetrator was not hard to find. He had panicked and run when he hit the container, and the police found him hiding in his parents' living room. His mother, whose car he had wrecked, was not very pleased!

Specific Locations

With the above context in mind, here are some specific types of facilities frequently used by multi-site churches. Each type comes with pros and cons that may require adjustments to your staffing, ministry options, and costs.

Schools

One of the greatest positives that churches with campuses in schools find is space — there is plenty of it. With cafeterias, auditoriums, and abundant classroom space, there are a variety of options for programming. On the flip side, housing a campus in a school can potentially limit your access to the space. Sometimes you can't get to the campus during special events or seasons of the year when the school, or portions of it, are unavailable. Also, churches often face limited flexibility when adjusting the layout of a room or making cosmetic alterations to the room to enhance the learning or worship environment. Sometimes these changes lead to conflict because of a school's rules or a teacher's desire to limit access to the classroom.

Schools are typically located in family-rich neighborhoods, making them a good magnet for attracting kids and their parents. The cost of using schools varies widely among districts, but it is generally quite reasonable when compared with that of other locations. School space is typically secured through an annual contract, with associated monthly fees. The key to effectively using schools for multi-site campuses is a high capacity for flexibility. Robert Emmitt says that at Community Bible, they are continually reminding their campus staff to always be ready for the unexpected.

YMCAs

There are many great reasons to use a YMCA for a multi-site church campus. The accommodations are often quite good — in terms of both space and design. The gymnasiums are often suitable for worship, and most YMCAs have smaller rooms that make great spaces for kids' and student ministry. Some YMCAs even have nursery space, designed for their "Mother's Day Out" programs, that is perfect for newborns and toddlers on a Sunday morning. Like schools, YMCAs are a great draw for kids, youth, and families.

The YMCA campus used by Community Bible Church in New Braunfels was previously an upscale fitness club. The facility is in great condition. On Sunday mornings, when the church has exclusive access, it's not unusual to walk by a bunch of treadmills en route to the worship space. Certainly, the location invites some great one-liners about getting in shape to meet with God!

The community-based locations of YMCAs also lead to opportunities for creative synergy between the YMCA and the church. Stillwater United Methodist Church has continued to develop their relationship with the YMCA that houses their second campus. The two organizations have a partnership that allows the YMCA to use the church for their daycare program. In addition, both now share a staff member — a leader who runs the YMCA's after-school mentoring program and works with junior high and senior high kids as the church's student pastor.

One of the biggest advantages to using a YMCA is often the price. The cost savings between renting a YMCA and renting other facilities are significant. Some have compared renting a YMCA with getting Saks Fifth Avenue quality at a Wal-Mart price. The arrangements are usually annually contracted, with monthly fees.

The greatest challenge that churches face when using YMCAs relates to time and availability. Most facilities open for business by one o'clock on Sunday afternoon, which can restrict the potential service times for the church. And as with many alternative locations, the weekly setup and teardown can, over time, be taxing on a team and lead to burnout.

EXAMPLES OF CHURCHES WITH YMCA CONNECTIONS

Community Bible Church	San Antonio, Texas	www.communitybible.com
Geist Christian Church	Fishers, Indiana	www.geistchristian.org
Life Church of Memphis	Cordova, Tennessee	www.thelifechurch.com
Lifespring Christian Church	Cincinnati, Ohio	www.lifespringchristian.org
Mary, Mother of the Church (Catholic)	Minneapolis, Minnesota	www.mmotc.org
New Hope Church	Manvel, Texas	www.newhopechurch.tv
Paseo Christian Church	El Paso, Texas	www.paseochristian.com
Stillwater United Methodist Church	Dayton, Ohio	www.stillwaterumc.org

Event Centers

Some of the most usable spaces for church campuses are centers for community-based events. They are designed for hosting events, their staffs are used to accommodating events, and they have great on-site storage. Because their program calendars often don't include Sunday events or have late-afternoon starts, these centers provide great flexibility in terms of setup and special programming needs. The greatest challenge when using these locations is the cost. They are typically one of the most expensive venues a church can secure.

Movie Theaters

Movie theaters can make great locations for campuses. They are often in very good locations, they are easily accessible, and people are used to going to them. The lobbies are bright and attractive. The auditoriums are comfortable and set up for good viewing from every chair. There is often space for storage behind the screen, or under the seat section if the theater has stadium seating. In some theaters, churches can utilize the state-of-the-art projection and sound systems.

However, theaters also present some notable obstacles. A church utilizing a theater has to exercise creativity when deciding how to set up an inviting nursery for small children. In addition, because the in-house acoustics are designed to deaden sound and because the rooms are intentionally dark, it is important to find the right sound reinforcement and add-on theatrical lighting to create an engaging atmosphere for worship.[8]

Community Recreation Centers

Community Bible Church opened one of its first multi-campus locations in the Wheatley Court Community Recreation Center. It was a part of Robert Emmitt's larger vision to serve the increasingly diverse community of San Antonio. They chose this location because of two benefits: the facility was free, and it provided an opportunity to serve a lower socioeconomic area of the city. But the challenges were also twofold. First, because the facility was community based, there was great competition with other groups for the space. Therefore consistency of use became a dream at best. The second and perhaps greater challenge was a cultural one. The very different demographic made it difficult to transfer the Community Bible Church DNA.

Renovated Retail Space

In terms of schedule, storage, and access, this is likely one of the best locations for a multi-site church campus. In most cases, you either own the space or have a long-term lease that provides you with exclusive access. The 24/7 access to the site affords the opportunity for using the space for midweek gatherings, leadership training, and staff offices. It also provides a sense of permanency for members and does away with the weekly setup and teardown regimen.

The biggest disadvantage when using retail space is the high cost. Even in areas where rental rates per square foot are low, the church must cover the additional build-out costs. These expenses can be quite high, and the long-term cost is often not recoverable. Churches that choose to purchase former retail space instead of leasing have both build-out costs and regular mortgage payments.

Though the costs are high for either of these scenarios, they are still typically less than those associated with new construction. Also, some churches have members with commercial real estate expertise who can scout out facilities and provide coaching should the church choose to lease or purchase these spaces. These members can be always on the hunt for spaces fit for a new campus or for an existing campus's next phase of growth. The advice they give can help the church design build-outs that both meet its needs and make the property most suitable for re-leasing or resale.

Why a Variety of Locations?

There are several strategies that multi-site churches can pursue as they consider operating out of diverse locations. The first is reactive—a church is experiencing rapid growth in worship attendance and needs to expand quickly. The demand for space forces creative solutions and ultimately leads the church to consider a variety of locations.

The other strategy is more proactive. It is driven by one or more of the following philosophies:

▶ *Diversification.* Operating in a variety of locations allows for diversification. Certain types of locations attract certain types of people. A church may choose to operate in a rehabbed downtown warehouse space to attract the young professionals living in gentrified urban neighborhoods. The same church might choose to set up a campus in a public school located in a suburban area of their community, to connect with the young families who have children attending that school. Different locations also lend themselves to varying worship styles and to creative opportunities for ministry beyond the primary worship gathering.

▶ *Partnership.* In some cases a church's commitment to multi-site is closely aligned with its value for presence in the community. This commitment may result in a partnership with a YMCA or a community center. Another expression of the partnership philosophy is found when churches choose to partner with state and local governments and create charter schools that serve the community and provide a shared facility for worship and ministry.

▶ *Locally owned.* A third reason why churches elect to operate in various locations is related to their desire to provide contextualized expressions of the original campus, particularly as campuses are being birthed in areas with a geographical spread greater than a specific metropolitan area. Facilities located in the next state or across the country may look different than the original campus because there are differences in local culture. The local context also takes into account economic and access factors. In some areas of the country, it is easier to gain access to schools, and in some places the costs of using a theater will be less.

As we emphasized in *The Multi-Site Church Revolution*, there is no one right way to do multi-site. Each church's vision, values, and context help it to shape the strategy that will have the greatest kingdom impact.

Location as a Third Place

Ray Oldenburg is credited with coining the term "third place" in his book *The Great Good Place*.[9] A third place is somewhere outside the first two spaces in our life: work and home. This principle was foundational in the early success of Starbucks. The founder affirmed that in addition to great coffee, the draw for Starbucks was the inviting environment provided in its retail locations. Many multi-site churches have been influenced by the third place idea as they have selected locations.

Ray Oldenburg believes that bars, coffee shops, general stores, and other third places are central to developing a vital community. Some call such places "social condensers" — places where community is developed, cohesion is retained, and a sense of identity is created. In the business world, the third place concept has become a buzzword for retailers as a "place to aspire to become."

Oldenburg lists the following eight characteristics of third places:

1. They are located on "neutral" ground.
2. They are "levelers" where rank and status don't matter.
3. Conversation is a main activity.
4. They are easy to access and accommodating.
5. They have a core group of influential regulars.
6. They have a low profile instead of being showy.
7. The mood is playful.
8. They feel like a home away from home.

Ed Stetzer, president of research with LifeWay Research, in a February 2008 study conducted for Cornerstone Knowledge Network, asked, "What kind of places do the unchurched like to come to?" The amount of people who chose a sit-down restaurant (47 percent) was more than three times the amount who chose any other site. Other locations that topped the list included a bar or nightclub (15 percent), a local coffee shop (13 percent), and a sporting event or recreational activity (5 percent).

According to the survey, the reason why people choose particular locations to meet with their friends is because these places are relaxing, casual, and fun. When asked to describe in their own words design features of the kind of place where they'd like to meet a friend, respondents mentioned a quiet environment, comfortable seating, and spaciousness and openness.

A church that embodies the idea of third place ministry is ReaLife Church in Philadelphia. ReaLife, planted jointly by Southern Baptist Church and the Acts 29 Network, started its church by purchasing a neighborhood bar. As in many urban contexts, it was a small bar that catered to the people who lived nearby.

In April of 2003, God provided the means for ReaLife to purchase Slugger's Bar in the church's target neighborhood. The first twelve months after the purchase were primarily consumed with the demolition and renovation of the bar into the newly established ReaLife Cafe. The cafe was established as a place for people from the surrounding communities to relax, have some coffee, and form relationships that explore faith and life. In addition, it became an intentional third place environment for outreach and community engagement.

Since the opening of the cafe in May 2004, ReaLife has used it to serve the community and build relationships in the neighborhood. Though God has brought many changes to ReaLife over the years, he has consistently confirmed their vision to meet the physical and spiritual needs of people in a way that reflects "real life" and leads to an ongoing conversation about issues of faith, God, and their relevance to the lives of people in the community.

But Not Just *Any* Space

A reporter from the *Chicago Tribune* recently asked me (Warren) if the rise in available real estate, from subleased movie theaters to vacant commercial properties, would spark the growth of new churches or multi-site campuses. My sense is that very few church leaders look at property and say, "Hey, it's for rent; let's start a church or add a campus there." Virtually every community has usable space where a church campus could meet. Available square footage is often not the main issue. Churches typically start new campuses because they are following God's call to reach people. The location is a means to an end.

Always remember that there is more than one way to start a multi-site church. Your church's vision, values, and specific context can help you shape the strategy that will have the greatest kingdom impact. You and your team will want to explore the variety of options in your community. Be sure to answer the "why" questions as well as the "where." Is your search for a new location a way of solving current space challenges, or is it part of your vision to extend the reach of your church into more diverse, unreached parts of your city? Do you want to create local ownership at your new campuses, or is your desire to form collaborative partnerships to address a specific need in your region?

As you consider a multi-campus extension, remember to stay close to God's heart for how he wants to use you in the surrounding community. In doing so, you will know which step of faith to take for your next location.

With that in mind, let's pack up our bags and head east to Baton Rouge, Louisiana, the home of Healing Place Church, a multi-site church whose compassion for the lost and hurting of their community has shaped a ministry that is transforming their city — and the world.

HEALING PLACE CHURCH

Baton Rouge, Louisiana

HEALING PLACE CHURCH

FAST FACTS

Church vision ► ***To be a healing place for a hurting world.***

Year founded ► ***1993***

Original location ► ***Baton Rouge, Louisiana***

Lead pastor ► ***Dino Rizzo***

Teaching model for off-sites ► ***Combination video/DVD and campus pastors teaching in person***

Denomination ► ***Nondenominational***

Year went multi-site ► ***2002***

Number of campuses ► ***11***

Number of weekly services ► ***18***

Worship attendance (all physical sites) ► ***7,200***

Largest room's seating capacity ► ***1,100***

Internet campus? ► ***Yes***

International campus? ► ***Yes***

Internet address ► ***www.healingplacechurch.org***

Multi-site churches are transforming their communities by contextualizing their service and outreach to the unique needs of each location.

One benefit of going multi-site is the opportunity it provides to make an impact on communities that others have overlooked or left behind. Some churches are opening campuses in decaying urban neighborhoods, while others are moving into economically underserved rural communities. While spreading the gospel, these churches are also addressing the tangible needs of people by giving out food, clothing, and free medical care to their new neighbors. To witness this movement in action, let's take a trip to the bayous of Louisiana and visit the home of Healing Place Church, headquartered in Baton Rouge.

There are three things you need to know about the staff at Healing Place Church. First, they love good food, and they do know what tastes good! Whether it's jambalaya, gumbo, or shrimp creole, the good old boys at Healing Place can hook you up with some good eats. I (Geoff) have learned one important lesson, though. When you eat there, don't ask too many questions about the ingredients in your stew. Chances are, it was frolicking in the woods a few hours before your meal!

The second thing you need to know about the staff at Healing Place is that they love the Louisiana State University Tigers. At the church, purple and gold is considered formal attire, and "Geaux Tigers!" is a standard greeting.

Apart from food and football, the most important thing you need to know about Healing Place's staff is that they love to serve people. Being a "healing place for a hurting world" isn't just a motto; it is at the heart of everything they do.

So it's not surprising that Healing Place doesn't view multi-site as a growth strategy; they see multiple locations as a way of meeting needs in more and more communities. Their goal isn't to build a really big church and attract lots of people; their focus is on transforming communities through no-strings-attached service done in the name of Jesus. They have coined the term "servolution" to describe their strategy for community transformation, and the senior pastor has even written a book with that title.[10] Currently this revolution of service in the name of Christ has spread to seven campuses in the United States and two locations in Africa.

The Vision Thing

At Healing Place Church, community transformation begins with a clear and consistent vision, a vision that hasn't changed since Pastor Dino Rizzo and his wife, DeLynn, started the church in 1993. The church began when the Rizzos shared their passion for ministry with then pastor John Osteen of Lakewood Church in Houston, Texas. After listening to their vision to serve the community, he gave Dino four hundred dollars and a mandate: "You need to start a church in Baton Rouge to reach the poor and hurting." That word confirmed for Dino what he felt God had been saying in his heart. Since that day, everything at Healing Place Church has been centered on taking care of the people no one else cares about.

> Everything at Healing Place Church has been centered on taking care of the people no one else cares about.

Dan Ohlerking, an assisting pastor at Healing Place, says that everything the church does is built around transforming the community. Whether they are engaged in disaster relief, opening a food pantry, or helping a single mom move her furniture, the goal of the church is community transformation in the name of Jesus. Dan says, "Serving is not just a piece of the church, a ministry, or a part of what we do; it is who we are. There is truth in the saying, 'Teach a man to fish and you feed him for a lifetime,' but there is also a time when you gotta just fry up some catfish and serve it to him."

Dan stresses that Healing Place doesn't just want to be a humanitarian organization. There are plenty of great humanitarian organizations out there doing good work, and Healing Place often partners with them. The distinguishing feature of Healing Place is that in everything they do, they do it in the name of Jesus. Dan says, "When you give a cup of water in the name of Jesus, there is a promise behind that. Whether you are teaching someone to fish or feeding them fish, you do it all in the name of Jesus. We go with the name of Jesus and the hope of Jesus. That's who we are."

Getting Started

When Healing Place goes into a new community, they look for the people in the gaps. They have discovered that there are many people who slip between the cracks in our society and have no organization, church, or government program helping them. These are the people Healing Place Church focuses on.

Over the years, the church has learned that when they begin to serve the least, help the lost, and meet the longings in a community, the community begins to respond — and change. Not everyone they reach out to is a single mom, a widow, or a homeless person, but everyone in the community knows someone who is. As Healing Place begins serving these forgotten people, the impact spreads beyond those they serve. From these simple beginnings, they sometimes decide to start a campus.

> When they begin to serve the least, help the lost, and meet the longings in a community, the community begins to respond — and change.

When assisting pastor Mark Stermer began helping kids in the community of Donaldsonville, one of the poorest zip codes in the nation, he wasn't planning on opening a Healing Place campus. Mark simply saw people in need and began figuring out how his church could help. One night, he heard about a family who had lost a close relative, so he and another pastor jumped into Mark's truck and headed over to the house to console them. On the way, he encountered a deer in the road that had been injured by a car. Mark jumped out of the truck, intending to scare the deer back into the woods, but he saw that it was severely hurt and unable to stand. Fortunately, Mark was prepared for just such an emergency. Pulling his hunting knife from the sheath hidden under his pants leg, Mark put the poor creature out of its misery, threw the carcass into the back of the truck, and continued on the journey. When they arrived at the house, the other pastor went inside to minister to the grieving family while Mark cleaned the deer in the yard. After the funeral the next day, the friends and relatives gathered for a meal of fresh venison with all the trimmings. Mark earned the nickname Deer Slayer that day—as well as the respect of the poor community he served.

After several years, Healing Place Church established a Dream Center in Donaldsonville, where they provided food, clothing, and resources for the underprivileged community. This center was based on an outreach model they had seen at Dream Centers in Los Angeles and Saint Louis. As they continued to serve the community, they also saw the need for a life-giving church. Since Mark was already serving in the community and was well known among the locals, he was chosen to be the campus pastor for the Healing Place Donaldsonville campus when weekend services were added at the Healing Place Dream Center. When Hurricane Katrina devastated New Orleans a few months later, this campus became ground zero for rescue and recovery operations for the hardest-hit neighborhoods. And it all started with a man with a heart to serve the people no one else noticed or cared about.

Dan Ohlerking offers two lines of advice for churches hoping to start a new campus in a community. First, you have to *be who you are*: outreach should be an authentic extension of your identity as a church and not just a program. Whatever you are is what you will spread in the community. If outreach and service aren't in the original church's

DNA, they will seem forced and disingenuous to people in the new community.

The second essential part of getting started is to *begin by serving within the community*—before you do anything else. Dan says, "Get yourself a great reputation in the community for giving to it, just being there to serve. Your heart cannot be, 'We want to put up another campus.' Instead your heart has to be, 'We want to reach that community.' You need to be okay with the idea that the community is worth serving even if you never open the doors to a campus there."

Contextualizing to the Community

In the early days at Healing Place, the church realized they could drive two miles in any direction in Baton Rouge and enter an entirely different culture. Rather than building one huge building and trying to get everyone to conform to the culture of the church, they decided to go into each distinct community in their area and contextualize what they did to the unique needs of that culture. The Donaldsonville campus is in a very poor neighborhood. Dan says, "It would not have worked for us to just bus them to the Highland campus [Healing Place's original location on Highland Road]. We always welcome

> "You need to be okay with the idea that the community is worth serving even if you never open the doors to a campus there."

them and at times even specifically invite them, but the backbone of it all is Healing Place's DNA being expressed in a way that is culturally applicable in their neighborhood."

Another Healing Place campus is located in Saint Francisville, home of Louisiana's state prison. This small, rural town is a tight-knit, traditional community of hunters and fishermen. A ministry that connects with the needs and interests of people at the Highland or Donaldsonville campus may be a complete miss in Saint Francisville.

Contextualization takes on an entirely different level of complexity at Healing Place's African campuses, located in Mozambique and Swaziland. Cheering for the Tigers to win the national championship means something completely different in the Louisiana bayou than it does in the African bush!

One way in which Healing Place is able to customize the experience at each of their campuses is through live teaching. All campuses are on the same page with Dino in the essentials of their teaching, but they are free to express the core message in a way that best relates to their community. Sometimes the messages are synched so every campus is preaching on the same topic; at other times pastors are given major themes for a series, and four or five weeks to cover those themes; and sometimes it is up to each campus pastor to decide what will be preached at his campus. The key for Dino is that the campus pastors share his heart. He calls it "presencing": when all the campus pastors share the same vision and passion for a message.

The campuses also sound different from one another. While many of the campuses use the same music, there is also variety among them. In addition to using contemporary worship, Donaldsonville will often throw in some more-traditional church tunes. The Saint Francisville campus weaves hymns among the Chris Tomlin and Dave Crowder tunes they typically sing. And in Baton Rouge, Pastor Fernando Gutierrez's campus sounds very different from the other campuses both in music and in language because his services are conducted in Spanish.

Even though each campus is contextualized to its community, the heart mission of Healing Place Church beats at each and every location: to be a healing place for a hurting world. From the inner city of Baton Rouge to the poor villages of Mozambique, the vision of the Healing Place campuses is to find ways to meet the needs of their neighbors. Communities in Africa have been amazed to see Healing Place members in Mozambique and Swaziland giving away food and expecting nothing in return. Everywhere Healing Place ministers, you can find evidence of a servolution.

Funding

Healing Place's strategy is more focused on meeting the needs of people in the community than on whether each campus is self-supporting financially. They tend to look more at the relationships they have in a community than at the balance sheet. Dan says they are looking for "the intersection of need and relationship."

At Healing Place, the original campus is seen as the *sending* campus. All the resources and material flow from Highland Road to the other campuses. Very few of the other campuses bring in enough money through offerings to break even on their budget.

Some of the funding for outreach at the various campuses comes through Church United for Community Development, a separate 501(c)(3) that Healing Place founded in conjunction with other churches in the area. Through this organization, they are able to apply for grants. They have received grants for a prisoner reentry program, ESL (English as a second language) classes, and after-school programs. Grants have helped Healing Place secure several fourplexes to serve as transitional houses for people in need of homes. After Hurricane Katrina, these apartments were used to house people displaced by the storm.

Dan says that other churches wishing to lead community transformation might want to investigate establishing a separate nonprofit in order to apply for grants. Healing Place found a volunteer at the church who had experience working with grants within the state educational system. Over recent years, she has secured millions of dollars in grants for a variety of ministries. "There is money available out there," Dan said. "For example, people have set aside money that they want to use to help inmates as they are released from prison. Why not use *that* money if it's a ministry you want to get started, rather than trying to figure it all out on your own?"

What's New about Multi-Sites and Community Transformation

Healing Place does a stellar job in reaching out and serving their community, and they regularly train other churches in community transformation, offering occasional "Experiences" for churches to come and learn firsthand. But Healing Place is not the only church to emphasize community transformation, nor the only multi-site congregation to do so. It is part of a national movement of churches that want to make a noticeable difference in their immediate community. Robert Lewis, former senior pastor of Fellowship Bible Church and lead author of *Church of Irresistible Influence* and *Culture Shift*, catalyzed the community transformation movement with his memorable question, "If your church suddenly disappeared, would anyone in your community be sad or weep that you're gone?" Pastor Rick Rusaw of Lifebridge Christian Church in Longmont, Colorado, popularized the term "externally focused church" through a widely read book of that name, coauthored with Eric Swanson. Reggie McNeal has advocated the phrase "missional church" through his influential books *The Present Future* and *Missional Renaissance.*

Led by the example of Healing Place Church and leaders like Reggie McNeal to invest additional resources and time into transforming our community, Seacoast Church decided to open our own North Charleston Dream Center in the fall of 2007. North Charleston, just across the bridge from the original Seacoast campus, is a racially mixed, lower-income community and is consistently named one of the ten most dangerous cities in America. Seacoast found a small church in the community that was willing to share their building, and we began reaching out to the neighborhood. We opened a food pantry and a clothes closet. We began offering ESL classes and tutoring in the local schools. On Saturdays we started going door to door, looking for ways to invest in the lives of neighbors.

The North Charleston campus has now moved into its own building and continues to distribute hundreds of meals, clothe dozens of families, and care for the needs of a struggling community. More than five hundred people attend weekend services, and in the spring of 2009 we opened a free medical clinic with a fleet of mobile medical units. As I (Geoff) can readily testify, all of this is about so much more than just the numbers. Seacoast is having a transforming impact on our community, making a real difference in the lives of people.

Multi-Site Benefits in Community Transformation

Whatever terminology you prefer to use, the key question to consider is this: does the multi-site model have advantages that can help your church become an agent for positive community transformation? We see three primary benefits for a multi-site church committed to community transformation, all of them modeled by Healing Place Church:

1. *Proximity.* Multi-site churches can go to where the people are. The motivating philosophy is not getting people to the church building; it's all about taking the church to the people by serving them and meeting practical needs.

2. *Resource allocation.* In many cases, multi-sites are more cost-effective than their single-location counterparts. Because the campuses of a multi-site church can pool their resources, their overhead is typically lower than that of a network of separate churches or that of a large, centralized location that uses shuttle busses or relies heavily on commuter transportation.

3. *Local Personalization.* Through multiple campuses, a church can have a Spanish flavor (and language) in one community, an urban flavor in another community, and a high-tech flavor in a highly wired suburb. All these approaches are motivated by an incarnational model that engages each local culture at its most receptive level.

Should You Open a Dream Center?

What would it look like if your next multi-site campus was a Dream Center? What would it say to the community if you moved into a neighborhood that other churches were leaving and decided to make a difference? Somewhere near one or more of your campuses, there are people who do not have enough food to eat, who do not have warm clothes to wear, or who lack adequate medical care. There are people in your community who desperately need to know that Jesus loves them and that he can set them free from the bondage in their lives. Serving others recaptures the original mission of Jesus, as he declared when he said, "The Spirit of the Lord is on me, because he has anointed me to preach good news to the poor. He has sent me to proclaim freedom for the prisoners and recovery of sight for the blind, to release the oppressed" (Luke 4:18). Community transformation begins with leaders who decide that their church will make a difference and take that first step. (For more information about the Dream Center organization, visit www.dreamcenter.org.)

As we continue on our roadtrip, we want to take a slight detour from the familiar roads we've taken so far. We've looked at what it might mean to serve those in our physical communities, but we now consider an entirely different type of community—the virtual one of the internet. What does it mean to serve people when you aren't physically present with them? One of the more intriguing developments over the past couple of years has been the proliferation of churches with internet campuses. For the next stop on our roadtrip, you'll need a computer and a high-speed internet connection. The good news is that you can go in your pajamas! Let's take a visit to one of these churches—online.

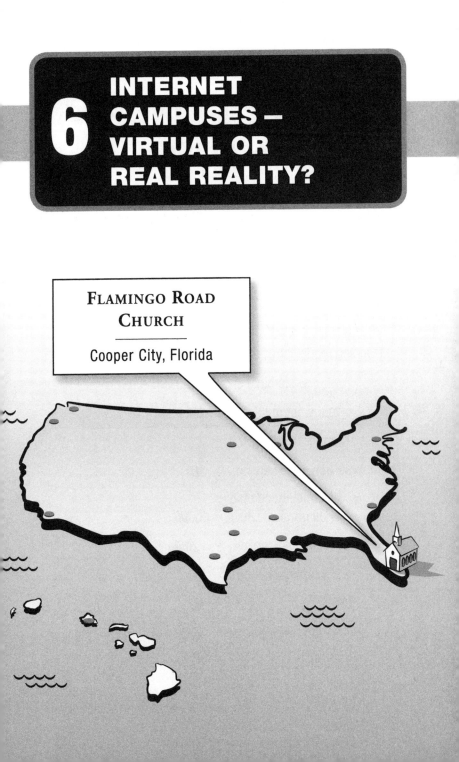

6

INTERNET CAMPUSES – VIRTUAL OR REAL REALITY?

FLAMINGO ROAD CHURCH

Cooper City, Florida

FLAMINGO ROAD CHURCH

FAST FACTS

Church vision ▶	**To partner with people to reach their God potential.**
Year founded ▶	**1981**
Original location ▶	**Cooper City, Florida**
Lead pastor ▶	**Troy Gramling**
Teaching model for off-sites ▶	**Primarily video/DVD**
Denomination ▶	**Southern Baptist**
Year went multi-site ▶	**2006**
Number of campuses ▶	**7**
Number of weekly services ▶	**20**
Worship attendance (all physical sites) ▶	**7,000**
Largest room's seating capacity ▶	**1,600**
Internet campus? ▶	**Yes**
International campus? ▶	**Yes**
Internet address ▶	**www.flamingoroadchurch.com**

While some debate whether an online campus is really a church, others see the internet as just another neighborhood, filled with people to be reached—and where you aren't limited by the size of a building.

At first, internet campuses were so unusual that they were constantly in the news. I (Greg) would read the reports with interest, wondering if this was for real. People claimed these things really worked! I imagined a scene with people laying hands on their computer screens, singing to themselves with eyes fixed on the monitor, hoping no one else could hear them. Four years later dozens of internet campuses now exist, some staffed full-time by pastors.

I'll be frank with you. I didn't expect to find much of genuine spiritual value in an internet campus. Sure, I constantly use the internet for my work. I am a frequent user of services like Twitter. I check email on my iPhone, and our sons Daniel and Andrew use the internet for everything from fantasy football to researching projects on Wikipedia. But I am also a people person, and I enjoy (and need) the connection that comes from sitting across the table from a good friend.

In the end, my curiosity overcame my apprehension and doubt, and I made my first visit to an internet campus. It really wasn't that difficult. I logged on to my computer, typed in a church website address, and clicked away. In fact, I'd like to invite you to take your own virtual roadtrip with me as I visit LifeChurch.tv, McLean Bible Church, and then Flamingo Road Church, all from the comfort of my home.

Surprising Responses

Churches began posting their service times on the internet in the mid-1990s, when everyone was learning how to get online. Soon churches were putting audios of their sermons online, and then videos of the service. As technology progressed, churches figured out how to stream their entire worship service live. There were times when I was traveling for a weekend and couldn't be present at our church, but I could "attend" by viewing or listening online. I thought the experience was an adequate substitute, but it still couldn't compare with being there live, in person.

And yet, besides the fact that I wasn't physically seated in the worship center with the families in our life group, my experience of worship on the internet was rather similar to the experience I have when I am inside a building at 201 Legacy Drive in Plano, Texas, with the marquee that says "Chase Oaks Church." With a fast internet connection, the music coming through my computer was strong, and it drew me into a "place" of connecting with God. I could listen to the message and think about how it applied to my life. Experiencing all this through a screen wasn't really a problem. After all, when I'm in our church's large auditorium in Plano, I watch our pastor on the projection screen—a real blessing to my over-forty eyes!

As the internet service continued, I found that still other facets of worship were present, including community activity announcements, prayers, and an opportunity to respond and interact with the message through the chat feature offered. If I desired, I could even participate in worship through giving my tithes and offerings ... online, of course.

I came to realize that many of my preconceived notions were formed from experiences with inauthentic, televangelist-preacher types from days gone by. But my experience at these virtual churches was quickly proving just how inaccurate those ideas were. Every one of the internet campuses I visited included both authentic teaching and an online campus pastor who was there to help me spiritually connect to the church.

One of my first online visits was to LifeChurch.tv, an innovative leader in the use of internet campuses. LifeChurch.tv launched its first internet campus in April 2006, and they now have a church on Second Life, the 3-D online virtual world. On Sundays LifeChurch.tv streams its service into a virtual Second LifeChurch.tv auditorium, where players can seat their characters, called avatars, and watch the sermon. In many ways it looks like a real church, complete with virtual donuts in the virtual lobby!

Another online visit took me to McLean Bible Church in McLean, Virginia, which launched its first internet campus in October 2007. On its debut Sunday, 356 people logged on to attend church online. The internet campus offered live streaming video of the worship (with lyrics) and teaching (with notes), a sermon notepad and relevant links, online giving, and the Lobby — a chat room where people from all over the world interact.

What Do Flamingos and Fort Worth Have in Common?

On a typical Sunday, while thousands of members of Flamingo Road Church make the literal trek from the parking lot to the auditorium for worship, Stephanie Smith grabs a cup of coffee and logs on to www.flamingoroadchurch.com. Stephanie lives in Forth Worth, Texas, fourteen hundred miles away from Cooper City, Florida!

Instead of attending a bricks-and-mortar church near her home, Stephanie hooks her computer up to her big-screen TV and watches a live webcast via Flamingo Road's internet campus. On some Sundays she invites her family and friends to join her.

Stephanie had been a member of Flamingo Road and attended services at the Florida campus until she was transferred to Texas. She didn't want to leave her church family, and thanks to their internet campus, she didn't have to. As she told a newspaper, "I still attend the services and still feel like I'm a part of everything that's going on with the church."[11]

Stephanie is one of a growing community of people who are connected to their church family through the internet. And *connected* is exactly what I felt when I logged on to the Flamingo Road internet campus! I attended church at Flamingo Road over several weekends, and then I contacted the church's senior pastor, Troy Gramling, to hear his behind-the-scenes story. I wanted to know what had led him to take seriously the idea of virtual, online community. "We went multi-site because we felt it was the best way to invest in people's lives to help them meet their God potential," Troy said. "In the same way, we added an internet campus because we felt it was the best way to invest in people's lives to help them meet their God potential. Everything we do is done because it helps people meet their God potential. If it ceases to meet that goal, we cease to do it." Troy believes that internet campuses present limitless opportunities for extending the reach of the gospel.

Troy's backstory made a lot of sense to me. He explained that as Flamingo Road Church grew, people were driving farther and farther to get to church. Soon the distance became a significant factor, limiting the ability of the church to effectively invest in people's lives. The church was experiencing some of the frustrations that are a common motivation for those who choose to go multi-site. Troy recalled the staff team saying, "We want to be involved with people where they live, where they play, where they work, where their kids go to school, and not everyone that we are reaching lives right here in Cooper City." Team conversation led to the launch of a multi-site ministry in February 2006. By early 2009 the church had seven campuses in a variety of locations, each seeking to figure out what the church's investment in people's lives should look like in their own neighborhood.

> Troy believes that internet campuses present limitless opportunities for extending the reach of the gospel.

Making It Work

As I explored the internet campus at Flamingo Road and at several other churches, I began to notice a number of important principles for developing a successful online church community. Those who wish to create these virtual communities need to know their neighborhood, carefully select the right technology, consider having an online campus pastor, and above all else be very clear and upfront about their connection process.

Know Your Neighborhood

As Flamingo Road became more comfortable with the reality of an online campus, they began to think beyond their immediate region. Soon afterward they found there was an opportunity to launch an additional campus — in Peru (for more on that story, see chapter 9). According to Troy, it wasn't until the launch of the Peru campus that they began to view the internet as a distinct region. He said, "We began to think about the internet as just another neighborhood filled with people — with the bonus that you are not limited by the size of buildings you have." By Troy's reasoning, while internet technology may be new, the idea of taking the church to the people is not. It's exactly what the apostle Paul and countless missionaries have done throughout the history of the church. Paul went to places like Ephesus and Corinth, where the people were open to hearing the Word of God, even receiving the message "with great eagerness" (Acts 17:11). Today some of those people are online.

Select Your Technology

Troy explained that they began the internet campus in much the same way as they started other initiatives. "We do very few things with a big, full-blown launch. We just started dreaming, and then as technology progressed and we had money to do new things, we gradually started developing it." They started simply, with streaming sermons, much as other churches were doing. This practice helped them develop some skill with the technology.

Then Troy went public with a sermon series entitled *The Naked Pastor*. It was a takeoff on reality television, supported by a real-time video cam that accompanied Troy through his week of interaction with his team, his family, and members of the church. "We knew we were on to something when we jumped to eight hundred online participants for that series," he says. "Regarding the technology we use, we started simple, and as new tools emerge that make sense for our model, we incorporate them."

Have an Online Campus Pastor

Flamingo Road took the next step in developing their internet campus by hiring a campus pastor, Brian Vasil, dedicated to the internet location. Brian had served for ten years on the church's video production staff. As pastor for the internet location, he disciples and cares for the folks who attend. Brian's team regularly talks about the importance of making sure people *participate* in the internet campus — not just watch or observe it. As Troy says, "We want them to feel that they are a part of Flamingo Road. We want them to know that we know they are 'out there' and that whatever we are doing as a church, they can participate."

Be Clear about Your Connection Process

Even if a church does a good job of creating an engaging and life-transforming online worship experience, it may not be enough. What about the rest of what it means to be the church? When I pressed Troy with this question, he said that both physical and internet campuses are trying to do the same thing: help people take the next step from where they are to where God is calling them. "The first step is accepting Christ," Troy explained. "That can happen anywhere. The next step is baptism, and we have discovered that can happen anywhere as well." Indeed, in 2007 Brian Vasil baptized a new believer online for the first time. They didn't use virtual water or a cheesy clip art graphic. It was the real thing.

A young woman from Georgia who had never attended any of Flamingo Road Church's physical campuses gave her life to Christ during a service on the internet campus. She wanted to be baptized, so she contacted her campus pastor, Brian, via email. He spoke with her on the phone about her decision to accept Christ and about her desire to be baptized. Then he helped coordinate the event. She was baptized by her mother-in-law in the family Jacuzzi tub with the Flamingo Road internet family watching via webcam and rejoicing in the significant moment for one of their peers. That's taking the next step. For those involved with the church, it was the real thing.

Troy indicated that the church's internet team gets emails and calls all the time about similar decisions in people's lives. He emphasized, "It's cool when you *see* people take those steps. Even though it is online, it provides the experience of being part of the community."

The next steps people are encouraged to take are bringing their lost friends to church and serving. The value of the internet campus in evangelism is immeasurable. And there are plenty of opportunities for people to serve, both virtually and in the physical neighborhoods of internet campus attenders. Online at Flamingo, people serve as greeters in the chat rooms. They pray with people following the services, and they do visitor follow-up during the week. These are just a few of the many opportunities to serve.

Some churches have even created scenarios that allow them to share in the sacrament of Communion online. Other churches are developing additional facets of ministry beyond weekend worship services. Some of the most promising initial developments have been in the direction of online small groups. Flamingo Road's online small group ministry comes live from Brian's home. Other churches have established online student and children's ministries where kids, students, and parents are engaging in the life of the church.

What Does an Internet Campus Cost?

The cost for an internet campus is basically whatever a church wants to spend. There are plenty of ways to stream live worship services for free, and some churches have begun describing that as their "internet campus." Other churches have a complete staff and a dedicated internet studio. Staff costs are typically the biggest factor. Sometimes a church decides also to pay for web development or for new equipment, such as additional cameras.

Why an Internet Campus Is Possible

One thing that makes participation in an internet campus even easier today than it was just five years ago is the reality that people are living more and more of their lives online. Many prefer internet shopping to bricks-and-mortar stores. They text their friends, send e-cards for birthdays, attend educational webinars, post comments on people's blogs, and share regular updates with Facebook or Twitter. The experience of sharing life together through an online neighborhood makes sense to a lot of people, and they have no difficulty applying the same experience to their desire for spiritual growth and community in the church. The emergence of the internet as a neighborhood of choice for millions of people opens up new opportunities for virtual multisite campuses.

Dave Kinnaman, president of the Barna Research Group, predicts that by 2010, 10 percent of Americans will rely *exclusively* on the internet for their religious experience. This includes listening to religious music, discussing religion in an online forum, or watching a video sermon on a topic that interests them at that particular moment.

> The emergence of the internet as a neighborhood of choice for millions of people opens up new opportunities for virtual multi-site campuses.

In addition to changes in mindset and patterns of behavior, the variety of readily accessible online tools makes interactivity and engagement with other people possible. Some churches keep it simple and embed a chat function on the internet campus site. Others are experimenting with video chat tools. Such technology can be used to create an "online lobby" where people connect before and after the services, and can even serve as a two-way communication tool with the campus pastor or other online church staff. Leaders of internet campuses have reported that many people have been led to Christ through the chat rooms of their sites.

Real Disciples? Handling the Skeptics

In a bricks-and-mortar church, leaders can limit distractions and use a variety of tools to create experiences to connect people emotionally to the music and message. With an online church, that is much harder to do. The people attending your church online might be doing a million different things in the background while the service is in progress. Or they might be in an environment filled with distractions. The growth edge for internet campuses is their need to move their attenders to full engagement. Perhaps the most challenging part of the internet campus idea is the reality that when people aren't physically in the room, as they are in a church sanctuary, you can't control the environment.

> The growth edge for internet campuses is their need to move their attenders to full engagement.

Some of you may still be skeptical (as I was before I experienced church online). The question asked most often is, "How do you know that disciples of Jesus Christ are actually being made?" When I asked Troy, he brought me back to his definition of church as a *process* of taking one step after another along the faith journey. As a church, Flamingo Road measures growth and discipleship through steps taken. Baptism is a discipleship step. Financial giving is a discipleship step. Serving is a discipleship step. Inviting friends to church and talking to them about Christ are also discipleship steps. Many of these discipleship steps are no different than the steps used to gauge growth at a church with a physical campus. In some cases they are even measured or tracked in the same way.

Troy sees the use of internet campuses as an outpouring of his pastoral heart. He views them as a tool to reach and disciple people all over the world. "Now it's hard for me to say I don't care about what happens in Oklahoma or Idaho or England or Peru," he says, "when I have the technology in my hands that can help me reach people in those neighborhoods."

Biblical Requirements for Church

Not everyone is quite as comfortable with the online approach to church. Mark Driscoll is the pastor of Mars Hill Church, which went multi-site in 1996 and currently has seven campuses in the Greater Seattle area. He objects to the idea of internet campuses, based on the definition of a local church found in Acts 2:42–47. Mark sees eight characteristics of a local church: (1) regenerated church membership, (2) qualified leadership, (3) preaching and worship, (4) rightly administered sacraments, (5) unity through the Holy Spirit, (6) holiness, (7) the Great Commandment to love, and (8) the Great Commission to evangelize and make disciples. "I believe technology is in no way a substitute for life-on-life, face-to-face, actual Christian community where the eight characteristics of the church are present," he says.

Even though he opposes the idea of the virtual church, Mark is certainly *not* opposed to the use of technology for ministry purposes. In 2007 Mars Hill Church was named the second most innovative church in America by *Outreach* magazine. In fact, Mark is very committed to the use of technology in ways that enhance and support actual, face-to-face community.

> Many of these discipleship steps are no different than the steps used to gauge growth at a church with a physical campus.

"At best, we might call an internet campus a ministry of a church, but to call it a church is without theological merit," he concludes. He acknowledges that there are certainly some people who cannot participate in regular church gatherings for valid health reasons, such as those who are hospitalized or the elderly. But he emphasizes as the norm Hebrews 10:24–25, which says, "Let us consider how we may spur one another on toward love and good deeds. Let us not give up meeting together, as some are in the habit of doing, but let us encourage one another." Mark is concerned that the American consumer mentality will lead people who are otherwise able to attend in-person church services to justify exempting themselves from the full experience of what God intends church life and church discipline to be.

Mark has also gone on record against the practice of counting online audiences as part of a church's regular attendance. He adds humorously, "That's as disingenuous as me counting the roughly ten million downloads of my sermons via the internet every year as my church and declaring myself the pastor of the largest church in the history of the world!" (We agree with him on this point and have used attendance totals only at physical church sites for our "Fast Facts" tables at the beginning of each chapter.)

Other Creative Ideas

The variety of ways in which churches with internet campuses use technology is "virtually" limitless. Here are a couple final insights and ideas for starting a campus online:

▶ *Sometimes in-person connections result from participation in the online experience.* Many internet campuses find that individuals are attending a weekend service online and then meeting in person during the week with a small group in their neighborhood. Other offline connections are found through serving opportunities in the geographic area where an internet campus member lives. Sometimes these connections are coordinated by the church, and at other times they are spontaneous as some of the individuals participating in an online worship experience discover that they share a zip code and a passion for a particular type of service.

▶ *Some churches use their internet campus as part of a launch strategy for a physical campus.* The internet campus allows a church to go somewhere before they actually "land on the ground" in the area. A good case in point is the Meeting

House. Their original campus is located in Oakville, Ontario, and they recently launched an eighth campus in Ottawa, a six-hour drive from Oakville. Virtually none of the people who first attended the Ottawa campus had any exposure to the physical location of the Meeting House in Oakville. The seeds of the campus launch came through people downloading podcasts of Bruxey Cavey, senior pastor of the Meeting House, and then meeting in home churches to discuss them. As time passed and the Ottawa community continued to grow, the church decided to add this location as a multi-site campus. Within five months of the launch, the campus had grown to more than fifty, and now has its own campus pastor. The success of this model could lead to campuses anywhere — Canada, the United States, or even Europe.

Your First (or Next) Internet Campus Visit

As you've probably noticed by now, each chapter in this book starts with a personal account of a multi-site visit. For this chapter, however, you can make your own site visit, and it won't cost you a dime (well, you'll need a computer and an internet connection). Type in www.multisiteroadtrip.com and look through the list of virtual churches in the sidebar, pick an internet campus to visit, log in, and prepare yourself to learn and grow deeper in your faith.

As you visit these internet campuses for yourself, you will probably need to wrestle with some of the questions raised by this new neighborhood. Learn how to use the tools that the church provides for connecting. Get to know the profiles of the people who "live there." Take some time to explore this new frontier. And as always, seek God for the direction he has for your church.

Well, it's time to get back on the road, this time with real pavement. Saddle up for a two-stop trip, first to North Coast Church just north of San Diego, California, and then back across the country to Edmond, Oklahoma, and LifeChurch.tv's original campus, where we will explore the headquarters of the multi-site technology capital of the world. (At least it is in our opinion!)

WHO IS DOING INTERNET CAMPUSES?

Brand New Church	Harrison, Arkansas	www.brand newchurch. com	iCampus
Celebration Church	Jacksonville, Florida	www.celebra tion.org	Internet campus
Central Christian Church	Las Vegas, Nevada	www.central christian.com	Online campus
Christ Fellowship	Palm Beach Gardens, Florida	www.gochrist fellowship.com	Live-streaming of worship services
The Church Group	Jacksonville, Florida	www.thechurch group.com	I-Church
Flamingo Road Church	Cooper City, Florida	www.flamingo roadchurch. com	Seven campuses, including an international campus in Lima, Peru. Also a blog (http://frclive. blogspot.com)
Gracepoint Church	Wichita, Kansas	www.grace point.com	Campus Connect, with live-streamed videos on Sundays
LifeChurch.tv	Edmond, Oklahoma	www. lifechurch.tv	Fourteen campuses in six states, including its internet campus and a campus in Second Life

Living Hope Church	Vancouver, Washington	www.living hopechurch. com/group/ lhc_internet	Internet campus worship
McLean Bible Church	metro Washington, D.C.	www.mclean bible.org	Multi-site campuses being launched around the Capital Beltway
New Hope Christian Fellowship	Honolulu, Hawaii	www.enew hope.org/live/	Online community
Northland, A Church Distributed	Orlando, Florida	www.north landchurch.net	Live web stream worship five times each weekend
Pine Ridge Church	Graham, North Carolina	www.pineridge church.tv	Worship on Sundays
Real Life Fellowship	Corpus Christi, Texas	www.reallife fellowship.org	Five sites on Real Life Online
Richmond Community Church	Richmond, Virginia	www.rcc-impact.com	Internet campus live on Sundays
Seacoast Church	Charleston, South Carolina	www.seacoast. org	Thirteen campuses in three states, including its internet campus
Victory Life Family Worship Center	Durant, Oklahoma	www.dsheriff. org	Virtual church where you can watch Duane Sheriff's messages 24/7 and live on Sundays

NORTH COAST CHURCH

Vista, California

NORTH COAST CHURCH

FAST FACTS

Church vision ▶ *To make disciples in a healthy church environment.*

Year founded ▶ *1978*

Original location ▶ *Vista, California*

Lead pastor ▶ *Larry Osborne*

Teaching model for off-sites ▶ *Video*

Denomination ▶ *Evangelical Free*

Year went multi-site ▶ *1998*

Number of campuses ▶ *5*

Number of weekly services ▶ *24*

Worship attendance (all physical sites) ▶ *7,500*

Largest room's seating capacity ▶ *560*

Internet campus? ▶ *No*

International campus? ▶ *No*

Internet address ▶ *www.northcoastchurch.com*

The infrastructure of a church that meets in multiple locations is often more about bandwidth and uplinks than about bricks and mortar. Balancing budget constraints and technological demands of several campuses is one of the more difficult challenges for a multi-site church.

North Coast Church, located just north of San Diego, was a pioneer in using video technology to expand the reach of the local church. When I (Geoff) first visited North Coast, I was impressed with the fun, almost carnival-like atmosphere at the church—as well as their effective use of low-cost technology. North Coast doesn't feel like a traditional church. Because it never rains in Southern California (according to a popular seventies tune), North Coast is able to utilize part of the parking lot of a light industrial park, where they are located, as their "lobby." Each unit in the complex houses a different video venue or children's classroom. Outside each venue is a brightly covered tent offering a variety of refreshments and resources. (One of the venues, called *The Edge*, offers free Mountain Dew in their tent. I know which venue I would attend if I lived in San Diego!)

On this 2004 visit, I was checking into North Coast's original auditorium, where they record the message that is later broadcast to the other venues. I was surprised to find a whopping grand total of one camera, and by no means was it top-of-the-line—it was a "prosumer"-level video camera. In the video venues, they were projecting the image from that single, standard-definition camera (as opposed to the high-definition image many churches use) onto moderately sized drop-down screens. There were no fancy graphics or cutaway shots to remind viewers that they're watching a video, just the single knee-up shot of teaching pastors Larry Osborne and Chris Brown. The projectors in each room were adequate but not overly bright. Overall, the technology was good enough to get the job done but not too impressive.

What *was* impressive was the engagement of the audience. Each venue I visited was at least 75 percent full, and in each auditorium, the attenders seemed as connected with Larry as if he had been in the room. They laughed, they nodded their heads, and they followed along in their Bibles. The lack of state-of-the-art technology did nothing to hinder the delivery of the message.

I should confess that at the time of my visit, North Coast was considerably more advanced than my own church, Seacoast. When Seacoast began using video teaching in 2002, we had two rules: it had to be low-cost—and it had to be cheap! Our initial solution was a single camera connected through an economical video switcher to consumer-grade S-VHS VCRs. After recording the service, we transported the tapes via Greyhound bus to our out-of-town campuses.

We inevitably ran into some challenges. S-VHS was a dying technology, and as we added campuses, it became more and more difficult to find enough VCRs to play our videotapes. Sending tapes by Greyhound was also becoming problematic. On more than one occasion our tapes went to Jacksonville, Florida, even though we didn't have a campus there. Campus pastors get very uptight when Sunday's message doesn't show up until the following Tuesday.

We knew we'd be forced to break both of our rules.

So began our quest for the perfect technology to complement a church with multiple locations. We knew there would be some bumps along the way, namely because the answer to the question, "How much do I have to spend on technology for multi-site?" is always, "How much do you have?" In other words, technology will always expand to fill any budget. There is always a better camera, a bigger switcher, or a faster connection.

Over the past few years, we have abandoned our VCRs and our late-night trips to the bus station, but to this day we continue our quest for the right technology. Another church that has been of significant help to us as we navigate the twists and turns of the digital pathway is LifeChurch.tv, based in Edmond, Oklahoma.

Serious, Intentional Technology

My first visit to LifeChurch.tv, in 2005, was for the final meeting of Leadership Network's initial Multi-Site Churches Leadership Community. We had been meeting with eleven other churches (including North Coast and LifeChurch.tv) over a span of two years, and I was curious to see in person what the people from Oklahoma were up to. I was also hoping to find some good Tex-Mex food (my life is a constant quest for the perfect meal). Since moving from Houston to Charleston in 1996, I had been severely deprived of even a decent bowl of chips and salsa. Jeff Kinney, who serves as the campus pastor of Seacoast's Irmo site, was a prior resident of Oklahoma City, and he assured us that Ted's Café Escondido would thrill even the most sophisticated Tex-Mex palate. Being a fajita snob, I doubted his word, but I confess I was wrong. Over the span of four days, we managed to visit Ted's three times. Their tasty chips and five kinds of fresh salsa were to die for!

Driving up to LifeChurch.tv's original campus, I knew we were in for a technological treat as well. Sitting prominently at the front of the building was a ginormous satellite dish — these guys weren't messing around! Inside the auditorium, we saw the largest video screen I had ever seen (at least without a hot dog in one hand and a big foam "Go Cardinals!" finger on the other). LifeChurch.tv was obviously miles ahead of Seacoast on the technology superhighway. Since my initial visit four years ago, LifeChurch.tv has remained at the cutting edge of church technology, so I thought a return roadtrip was necessary to help us answer the four major technology questions every multi-site church has to tackle (and to get more of Ted's salsa and chips).

1. How Do We Connect Our Campuses?

When everyone in a church shares the same office space, lives in the same community, and attends the same services on the weekend, connection is fairly easy. But when you open up multiple locations in multiple cities in multiple states, things can get very difficult. Having the right technology can help reestablish that tight connection between locations. Most multi-site churches find it helpful to utilize a mix of conference calls, videoconferences, VPNs (virtual private networks), and intranet sites to link campuses together, but LifeChurch.tv has taken campus connection to a whole new level with their Global Operations Center (GOC).

Located in a conference room on the second floor of their Edmond campus, the GOC looks like a smaller version of NASA's mission control. Projected on one wall is a matrix of live feeds from various LifeChurch.tv campuses. (The portable campuses aren't currently connected to the GOC.) Next to the matrix you'll find screens with real-time updates listing the weekend attendance at each campus, as well as other crucial measurements fed by LifeChurch.tv's Church-Metrics software (www.churchmetrics.com). In the middle of the room is a large conference table with several audio stations. At each station, a user can listen in on any one of the individual "experiences" (their term for worship services) live at any LifeChurch.tv campus. Each experience is recorded and can be viewed at any time.

Sunny Thomas, technical director for LifeChurch.tv, says the GOC allows the directional leadership team to use technology in ways that offer better support to the ministry happening at the campuses each weekend. This helps the leadership team make better decisions. Youth leaders also utilize the GOC to get a feel for what is happening in the youth ministries at each campus, by observing their experiences that occur midweek.

Another advantage of the GOC is the ability to give instant feedback. The campus pastor in Tulsa might do an amazing job with the wrap-up at one of the weekend experiences. Someone watching in the GOC can relay how he handled the conclusion to the other campus pastors so they can incorporate that into their next experience. When I visited the GOC, Sam Roberts, campus operations pastor, saw that one of the video elements that the campus pastors had set up for that weekend needed to be tweaked. He was able to text the change to all the campus pastors before the start of their next experience. He also texted several guys, giving them instant encouragement and feedback relating to the events happening at their campuses. There was definitely a "one church, many campuses" environment in the GOC that weekend.

After our team at Seacoast visited the LifeChurch.tv GOC, we liked it so much that we decided to build our own. We installed security cameras at each of our permanent locations and connected them to our original location via the internet. We are now able to zoom, pan, and tilt the cameras remotely so we can get a feel for audience participation as well as what is happening on the stage. The system was affectionately dubbed Big Brother by some of the campuses, but we call it the Skybox. Once we got past the creepiness factor, the Skybox has become a tremendous tool for sensing the connection among the campuses. As great as these technologies are at providing us with a sense of real-time connection to our campuses, Sunny Thomas at LifeChurch.tv was quick to caution us that the GOC or Skybox is not a substitute for campus visits. It's just another tool that helps us build connections among sites.

2. How Do We Capture Our Content?

For churches that use in-person teaching at every site, capturing content is not a big challenge, but for churches with video venues, image capture can be one of the biggest expenses. Options for capturing video range from Uncle Sid and his 1985-era VHS home video camera to the latest holographic technology. In addition to budget considerations, there are several questions a church has to wrestle with in deciding how they will record their weekend services:

▶ *What is the audience where the content will be played?* The issue here is who will be watching the service. There are many possibilities. Will it be a college student watching on a computer screen in her dorm room? A small group gathered around a television in a living room? Fifty people in an on-site overflow room? Two hundred people sitting in a darkened theater? One thousand people in a converted grocery store? As a general rule of thumb, the larger the potential audience, the more sophisticated the recording quality needs to be. Uncle Sid's camera may work for the college student watching on a laptop, but the large audience in the converted grocery store will need a significantly higher level of quality and resolution.

▶ *What are the expectations of the audience at the video venue?* One of the major questions a church using video venues has to ask is whether it will capture content in standard definition (SD) or high definition (HD). As people become more accustomed to HD content in their home, they will begin to expect that level of quality wherever they go. Many churches are finding that SD is becoming a barrier for people coming into a video venue for the first time. On the positive side, the cost of HD capture and playback has continued to drop dramatically year after year.

▶ *What is the expertise of the staff and volunteers who will be operating the cameras and video switcher?* The biggest key for effective capture is having the right people turning the knobs and pushing the buttons. The more a church relies on volunteers for their video ministry, the simpler their system needs to be. Three manned HD cameras running through a complex video switcher can lead to horrible disasters in inexperienced hands.

> The larger the potential audience, the more sophisticated the recording quality needs to be.

LifeChurch.tv currently records their weekend services at their broadcast facility using four Panasonic HD cameras. Two cameras are manned, and two are controlled remotely. The content is output three ways for redundancy: they capture to two Apple Xserves using Gallery PictureReady digitizing stations, and they also utilize a Panasonic DVCPro tape deck.

Seacoast's current system is a little simpler, and it's the same technology we've used for the past six years. We use a manned Ikegami

SD camera and a remotely controlled Sony SD camera. We record simultaneously to a Panasonic DVCPro tape deck, a Panasonic DVD recorder, and a Telestream Clipmail video encoder.

3. How Do We Distribute Our Content?

Since we abandoned the Greyhound bus system, Seacoast has been on a quest to find the perfect distribution system. Currently all twelve of our off-site campuses use the sermon content recorded the prior weekend, so we are able to FedEx DVDs to all the distant campuses. For redundancy, we also send our content over the internet via FTP (file transfer protocol, designed for huge files) to many of our campuses. On weekends such as Easter, when all campuses need to be synchronized, we record the message on Saturday night and then send couriers to every campus. It's not a sophisticated system, but it is better than having our campus pastors sitting at the Greyhound station at 2:00 a.m. on Easter Sunday morning.

LifeChurch.tv distributes their weekend content via satellite. They have an uplink dish at their original Oklahoma location, where the teaching pastor, usually Craig Groeschel, speaks live most weekends. Each permanent location has a smaller downlink dish, so the message is played live at most of them. Sunny Thomas lists several advantages for distributing their content live via satellite:

- ▶ With all campuses seeing the same message each weekend, the whole church is moving in the same direction at the same time.
- ▶ There is less financial overhead once the initial uplink equipment is purchased. Downlink equipment is typically less than five thousand dollars per site, and LifeChurch.tv has to pay for satellite time only *once* regardless of the number of campuses that tune in.
- ▶ All of the collateral material at each campus is the same. This would include bulletins, children's handouts, and promotional signage. It is less complicated to have all the campuses on the same page at the same time.

Sunny does agree that satellite broadcasting adds a level of complexity to the weekend and there is far less room for errors. LifeChurch. tv offers a 5:00 p.m. Saturday experience at several campuses, and there is no backup available if something goes wrong with the satellite transmission. In that case, the campus pastor would generally finish the message based on notes received earlier in the week. Each campus records the 5:00 experience to use as a backup in case there is a technical problem with any of the other experience times during the weekend. For campuses without satellite capability, the Saturday night message file is sent electronically overnight to the campus, burned to a DVD, and also recorded to a LaCie Multimedia Hard Disk. The DVD and hard drive file are played back simultaneously on Sunday.

So with all this in mind, should your church use satellite technology to distribute your content? The answer to that question depends on several factors:

▶ *What is your budget?* Satellite has relatively high setup costs, and satellite time will cost at least three hundred dollars per hour every weekend.

▶ *How many campuses do you plan to open?* Unless you plan to have four or more campuses, there are simpler and more cost-effective ways than satellite to distribute your content.

▶ *How widespread are your campuses?* When Perry Noble began a Bible study in his living room in Anderson, South Carolina, he never imagined it would grow into NewSpring Church, with over ten thousand attenders every weekend. Soon after moving into their first permanent building in 2006, New-Spring was out of room, so they decided to open a campus thirty miles up the road in Greenville. Perry wanted a live experience at both campuses, so the decision was made to utilize a Metro E fiber connection between the original location and the renovated grocery store in Greenville. NewSpring streams both a live HD lockdown shot projected on a large center screen and an SD shot for close-ups projected on two side screens.

4. How Do We Play Our Content at the Campuses?

To keep things as simple as possible, LifeChurch.tv projects the same image on three screens at all of their campuses (rather than projecting two different shots, as they do at NewSpring). LifeChurch.tv primarily uses 10' x 17' center screens and 8' x 14' side screens illuminated by Panasonic 7000 and 5100 projectors. For redundancy, messages are played back simultaneously from a satellite receiver, a DVD, and a LaCie hard drive. The theory is that there is very little chance that all three will fail at the same time.

At Seacoast, we also project a single image on three screens. At some campuses, we have only one large screen. We normally use a waist-up shot for the message. We have found that with the size of our screens, this close-up shot works best. Churches utilizing HD and huge center screens usually use a full-body, slightly larger-than-life shot, giving the impression that the speaker is on the stage.

Seacoast plays the message simultaneously from a hard drive video device and two DVDs as backups. Our campus pastors also get a copy of the teaching pastor's manuscript so they can finish the message in case all else fails. We have had to go to the live campus pastor on only a few occasions.

Starting Simple

I (Warren) served on the staff of a medium-size church that experimented for several years with multiple venues. It all started when we noticed that there were a dozen or so people hanging out around a certain coffee pot during the services. Each week they would linger in a hallway that had some comfy chairs nearby and then circle them together. We eventually figured out how to send a camera feed to a big television screen there so the coffee pot crowd could enjoy the service. I wish we had kept a photo of the camera control room. Geoff's Uncle Sid would have admired the way we jerry-rigged our donated equipment to get those video and audio signals over to this coffee gathering. We later tried several other experiments using the church chapel for live worship music followed by a TiVo (time-delayed) version of the message from the sanctuary.

I've been to other churches that made the transition to multi-site on a frugal budget, creatively using the equipment they had. According to our research at Leadership Network, churches are roughly divided into thirds when it comes to the teaching message:

▶ One-third of churches use only video teaching for their off-site campuses.

▶ One-third use only in-person teaching for their off-site campuses.

▶ One-third use some combination of both video and in-person teaching for their off-site campuses.

Interestingly enough, those ratios tend to change with church size. Churches often begin using more video teaching (a) as combined attendance increases and (b) as the number of campuses increases. If you think about it, there is a certain logic to it. The majority of multi-site churches in the United States have just two campuses, and these are often relatively close to one another. This makes it fairly easy to have the lead pastor teaching at one campus and an assisting pastor at another. Sometimes there is a staff rotation between the two campuses. Either way, with two campuses it's possible to have in-person teaching with minimal disruption.

The challenge to in-person teaching often comes when you go past your third campus and begin launching four or more. It's much more difficult to coordinate the pastors and get them together to plan and prepare a message. At that point, churches will often begin using more video or satellite teaching options. Also, by that point most churches are large enough to hire media specialists onto their staff. If the media equipment is 1 percent of the church budget and the church is larger, the 1 percent can now buy the equipment necessary to do video teaching.

Your Next "Fun" with Technology

There once was a time when the idea of installing indoor plumbing in a church was considered innovative—and controversial. Churches have come a long way since the days of arguing over whether to use ministry money for that newfangled plumbing technology called a bathroom. The same was true when churches had to decide whether or not to have a kitchen in the church building or install a telephone line or an answering machine, get a beeper for the pastor, a fax machine for the church office, a sound board for the sanctuary, or a light mixer for the youth group. All of these technologies, when they were new, led to some major discussions and in some cases extensive arguments over the best use of church funds.

Today technology is used not simply for worship services; it is also essential for communicating with staff and engaging in ongoing leadership development, as some of the later chapters will describe. For multi-site contexts in particular, you might want to stop and go through the four questions outlined earlier in this chapter. You might want to gather your tech team volunteers and staff together for a dream-it day to discuss the questions, "What new technologies on the horizon could we harness for kingdom use within current fund limitations?" and "What are other churches experimenting with that we might explore, budget permitting, for reaching more people and for making more and better disciples of Jesus Christ?"

After you spend some time dreaming, you can Twitter, podcast, or blog your insights so others can benefit—that is, unless those technologies are already obsolete! Regardless of the technology you choose to use, there is at least one constant of multi-site church ministry—you'll have to constantly adapt and change your structure. In the next chapter, we will visit the windy city of Chicago and learn from Community Christian Church what they have found about the importance of structuring a multi-site church for growth, and the ongoing adaptations that have been required.

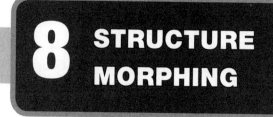

8 STRUCTURE MORPHING

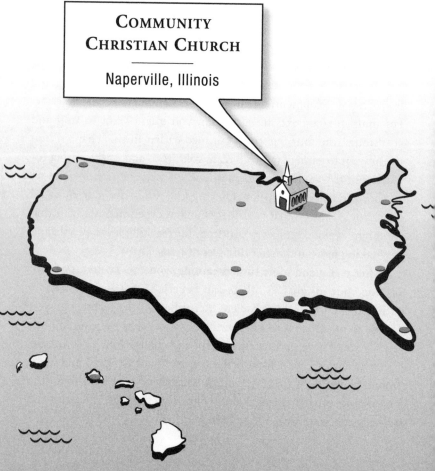

COMMUNITY CHRISTIAN CHURCH

Naperville, Illinois

COMMUNITY CHRISTIAN CHURCH

FAST FACTS

Church vision ▶ **To help people find their way back to God.**

Year founded ▶ **1989**

Original location ▶ **Naperville, Illinois**

Lead pastor ▶ **Dave Ferguson**

Teaching model for off-sites ▶ **Combination video/DVD and campus pastors teaching in person**

Denomination ▶ **Nondenominational**

Year went multi-site ▶ **1998**

Number of campuses ▶ **9**

Number of weekly services ▶ **24**

Worship attendance (all physical sites) ▶ **5,158**

Largest room's seating capacity ▶ **550**

Internet campus? ▶ **No**

International campus? ▶ **No**

Internet address ▶ **www.communitychristian. org**

When a church goes from one campus to many campuses, its organizational chart is stretched to the breaking point. The ability to reorganize quickly is an important skill in the multi-site church toolbox.

One of the questions we most often hear from churches considering a multiple-location model is, "What is the best structure for a multi-site church?" In many ways, that's like asking whether to buy a small, medium, or large when purchasing a T-shirt. It all depends on the size of the body! One thing is always true: adding locations will mean changing the way you are organized.

Dave Ferguson and his team at Community Christian Church (often abbreviated CCC because these letters also represent the church's foundational values of celebrate, connect, and contribute) have done some of the best work addressing the question of multi-site church structure, so let's head out to the suburbs of Chicago to learn from their insights. When I (Geoff) drove up to CCC's original site in Naperville, Illinois, my first thought was, "What an enormous yellow box!" The church building was big and square and, unlike any church I had seen before or since, decidedly yellow. I soon found out that CCC affectionately (and creatively) refers to the building as the Yellow Box. Despite its yellow exterior, this distinctive landmark houses some of the most courageous pioneers of the multi-site movement — not to mention a rather amazing congregation.

Dave (who turned me on to an amazing little bistro in downtown Naperville named LaSorella DiFrancesca) launched CCC in 1988 with his younger and taller brother Jon and a group of friends. Their vision was to plant a "new thing" in the Greater Chicago area. When in 1998 a builder in the congregation offered them an opportunity to move into a community center he was planning in nearby Romeoville,

CCC expanded to a second site. Jon Ferguson soon became the Yellow Box's campus pastor, and Troy McMahon became the campus pastor of the new Romeoville location—a community center in the heart of a housing complex. Subsequent campuses were launched in the community center of a gated retirement community, in dying churches that merged with CCC, and in public schools. In addition, CCC has helped birth more than twenty new congregations through the New Thing Network.

Whether you are opening your first off-site location or, like CCC, you have almost as many campuses as Baskin-Robbins has flavors, the structure of your church is a constant challenge. In our first book, *The Multi-Site Church Revolution*, we profiled the basic structure of a typical multi-site church as it adds new sites. Here we want to take another look at five structure questions that every multi-site church must answer with every new site they start. We'll answer these questions through the experiences of Community Christian Church, Seacoast, and LifeChurch.tv.

Who Makes the Decisions?

Suppose you are launching a new campus in Cut n Shoot, Texas (an actual town near a church I once pastored). Who will call the shots at your new campus? Are your staff members free to hold a Holy Ghost Hoedown and Hallelujah Stomp-fest, or do they need to first run it by a central board?

On a more serious note, what level of the church's leadership needs to authorize the strategic green move from incandescent bulbs to power-saving fluorescent lights? Can one of your campuses with a thriving, exploding youth ministry hire a new youth pastor? Can they fire him six weeks later when he sets off the fire alarm with a smoke machine and shuts down an entire strip mall where they're renting? (Sadly, that one is an actual Seacoast story.) Deciding who makes the big decisions, the small decisions, and all the decisions in between is a major part of getting the structure question right.

At CCC, the campuses are grouped into two regions, each led by a regional pastor who is also a campus pastor at one of the nine sites. Each campus, then, is led by a pastor who is responsible for the decisions that impact his individual site.

When I asked Jon about the level of freedom their campus pastors had to make decisions, he admitted that the issue has been a challenge from the beginning. "That's been huge for us. Everything at CCC rises and falls on our campus pastors. The only way to get the best leaders is if they feel like they can create and execute the vision in a way they can make it their own. But we would get these great leaders and tell them, 'Do whatever you want—except for that, and wow, not that either.'"

To help give their campus pastors freedom with fences, CCC created their campus constants, basic standards for the main ministries of a CCC:

Ten Campus Constants at Community Christian Church

1. Mission: Helping people find their way back to God.
2. Vision: Embrace the churchwide vision each year with some room for appropriate modifications that account for various campus life-stages.
3. 3C's: Celebrate, Connect, and Contribute serve as the foundation for spiritual growth.
4. Big Idea: One "Big Idea" for adults, students, and children will be executed weekly.
5. Teaching Team: The teaching team will set the teaching schedule and will serve as the primary communicators, either in person or by videocast.
6. Leadership Structure: There is one leadership structure with coaches, leaders, and apprentice leaders.
7. Leadership Community: There are monthly gatherings of leaders for vision, and skill development. This takes place at a central location.

8. Financial Model: Follows a 70/20/10 pattern, with each campus operating on 70 percent or less of its offerings within five years of a launch. Twenty percent or less of campus offerings will be used to support the catalyst organization, and 10 percent will be used for new churchwide endeavors.

9. 3C/MS: One centralized database for people, groups, events, and finances is used to measure a site's 3C status.

10. Central Services: One centralized process or system is used for business services: banking, staffing, payroll, benefits, capital expenditures, lease agreements, etc.

Jon says, "Our campus constants became the fence around the playground. The campus pastors now have the freedom to dream and create a unique vision of their campus within the parameters set in advance."

> "The campus pastors now have the freedom to dream and create a unique vision of their campus within the parameters set in advance."

Do You Need a Central Support Team?

At the start of our multi-site journey at Seacoast, our central support team consisted of me (Geoff), my incredible assistant Lori Fitzgerald, and uber-volunteer Byron Davis. The structure was simple enough: Byron handled all the money questions, I handled all the ministry questions, and Lori handled everything else. For most churches that have one campus with multiple venues, two campuses, or even three campuses, this can work quite well, especially if you find and train people as competent as Lori and Byron.

Our simple structure was designed to keep everything from falling on the senior pastor. It gave our campuses a consistent point of contact for each type of question, someone they knew personally, someone who had time to make their concerns a priority. In those days I did a lot of site visits, and our campus pastors came regularly to our Mount Pleasant office.

We were a manageable family—until more children came along.

Once we reached four campuses, our structure became completely insane. Staff would phone Byron, email me, and text Lori—all with the same question. If we didn't get back to them fast enough (within fourteen minutes), they would simply go find someone else who might have the answer. Or they'd just do whatever they wanted to do in the first place. The motto for our staff became, "It is easier to ask forgiveness than permission."

At that point we decided to create a real central support structure. We centralized all the IT, accounting, and HR functions for the church. We moved several of our best leaders from hands-on ministry to central support roles. No longer did every question get funneled to one of three people. We now had a plethora of staff who were somewhat stunned and confused, but they did their best to be helpful.

We ran into several challenges at this stage of growth. First, it became very expensive to maintain staff at each campus in addition to staffing the central support. Second, we had moved some of our best leaders from the front lines of ministry without providing equally qualified replacements, and some of the ministries suffered as a result. Finally, the leaders who used to be knee-deep in hands-on ministry every weekend were now relegated to support roles. They missed the connection with the volunteers and people, and we began to see some of our central staff dying on the vine.

We settled on a compromise. We kept senior leadership and all the administrative roles in central support, but we returned almost all of our ministry people to roles within specific campuses so they could impact day-to-day ministry. Today our structure looks somewhat like the figure on the following page.

How Do Ministries Interrelate?

Another challenge for multi-site churches is how the ministries relate to one other. Does everyone use the same children's curriculum? Do all the campuses sing the same worship songs? Who makes these kinds of decisions? Who makes sure everyone is on the same page

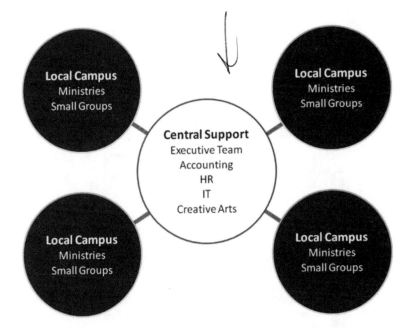

and working together? With one, two, or even three campuses, the answer is often relatively simple. If you're together enough in person and you communicate well with each other, you can handle these issues at a rate that doesn't challenge anyone's sanity. One of several possible structures can work, as long as you're consistent and you communicate clearly.

But what happens when you go to four or more campuses? How can the ministries continue to interrelate well with each other? Like other churches that now meet in many different locations, CCC has struggled through the challenges of structuring multiple sites and has evolved through the years as the church became more complex in size and scope of ministry. In the early years, everything at CCC was divided into three broad categories: arts, business, and community. The ministry leaders at the campuses reported to the appropriate director in their category area rather than to a campus pastor. So the music leaders at each campus reported to the arts director (under the arts category). The children's leaders reported to the children's ministry director (under the community category). It looked like this:

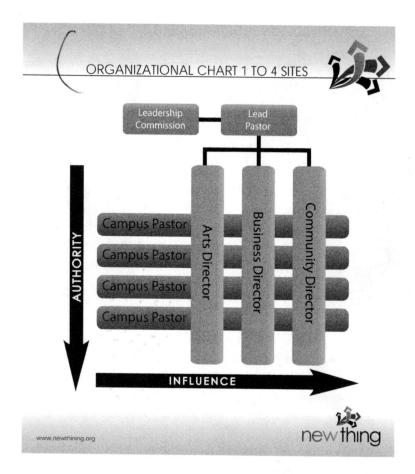

ORGANIZATIONAL CHART 1 TO 4 SITES

Leadership Commission — Lead Pastor

AUTHORITY

Campus Pastor
Campus Pastor
Campus Pastor
Campus Pastor

Arts Director
Business Director
Community Director

INFLUENCE

www.newthing.org

new thing

One of the reasons why this arrangement was effective for many years at CCC was the proximity of the staff. For the first several campuses, everyone had an office at the Yellow Box. In truth, everyone had an office in the same big open room. So they functioned as one big staff, talking with each other constantly, even though they had responsibilities at different campuses on the weekends. As CCC continued to grow, however, the church realized that the campus pastors needed more authority to impact what was happening week after week on their own campuses. In addition, the staff ministry leaders were being stretched to the breaking point as they worked across multiple campuses. So the decision was made to change everything by flipping the structure around. The shift gave authority to the campus pastors so they could now oversee the ministry staff assigned to their location. The children's ministry director at the Naperville campus now answered directly to the Naperville campus pastor rather than to the community director. A new position called "champion" was added as well. The champion would be a person with the capacity and expertise to both lead an area of ministry within a campus and influence the philosophy, personnel, and programming of that ministry across all the campuses. According to Jon Ferguson, champions actually function more as consultants for the church. They are responsible for the overall direction of the ministry, and they help ensure that every campus looks and feels like Community Christian Church.

With this shift, the authority in the church was now flowing through the campus pastors, but the primary influencer in the church was now the ministry champion. At the Romeoville campus, the children's ministry director was now answering to Troy McMahon, the campus pastor, but she was taking her lead for the overall direction of the children's ministry from Tammy Melchien, the children's ministry champion.

CCC also added a third layer of structure to the relationship among ministries, with the role of "catalyst." Just as the champion is primarily concerned with the proper alignment among campuses, and the ministry director is focused on recruiting and executing, the catalyst in each ministry area is responsible for development and distribution of products and resources. CCC's current structure looks like the figure on page 124.

How Does the Campus Pastor Thing Work?

The role of campus pastor is unlike any other staff position at a church. Campus pastors lead an entire campus, but they aren't free to make their own decisions in the same way a solo pastor would. Their job is to spread the vision of a senior pastor, whom they may talk with in-person only about once a month. In a video-driven ministry, the

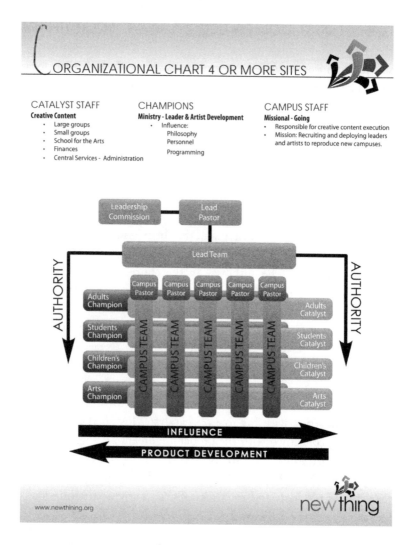

ORGANIZATIONAL CHART 4 OR MORE SITES

CATALYST STAFF
Creative Content
- Large groups
- Small groups
- School for the Arts
- Finances
- Central Services - Administration

CHAMPIONS
Ministry - Leader & Artist Development
- Influence:
  Philosophy
  Personnel
  Programming

CAMPUS STAFF
Missional - Going
- Responsible for creative content execution
- Mission: Recruiting and deploying leaders and artists to reproduce new campuses.

Leadership Commission — Lead Pastor

Lead Team

Campus Pastor | Campus Pastor | Campus Pastor | Campus Pastor | Campus Pastor

AUTHORITY

Adults Champion — Adults Catalyst
Students Champion — Students Catalyst
Children's Champion — Children's Catalyst
Arts Champion — Arts Catalyst

CAMPUS TEAM

INFLUENCE →
PRODUCT DEVELOPMENT ←

www.newthining.org

new**thing**

campus pastor is expected to cast vision, touch hearts, and cover the announcements in perhaps 240 public seconds or less each weekend. That takes a special set of gifts!

Every multi-site church eventually has to make a decision about their site leadership: what is the role of the campus pastor?

One of the first things CCC did when they opened their second campus was to appoint a campus pastor at their *original* location. In this way, they have one person at every campus whose responsibility upon waking up each morning is to think about the people and ministry of that particular campus. This structure frees the senior pastor to give oversight to all campuses—and to the church as a whole—even while still being primarily based at one location.

At Seacoast, our senior pastor served as the campus pastor at our Mount Pleasant site (our original one) until the opening of our fourth location. Why did he wait so long? I think he delayed for the same reason many other senior pastors wait: they try to fill both roles (overseeing the entire church while caring for one particular campus) because it's just really hard to let go! It is often tough for senior pastors to release to a new leader a ministry they have overseen for several years. We admit that all this is still a work in progress at Seacoast, and the same is true at most multi-site churches I have talked with. But in the end, there are several advantages to releasing the role sooner than later, the main one being that the campuses seem more balanced. Instead of one campus serving as the "premier" location for the church, with the others functioning as second-class satellites, you have a sense of unity and equality among the campuses.

Once a church transitions the senior leader away from the campus pastor role, how does that leader continue to connect with the other campus pastors? At CCC, until recently the campus pastors all met with senior pastor Dave Ferguson weekly. Eventually it all became overwhelming. There were far too many people in the room for any sort of meaningful dialogue, and Dave couldn't give adequate, individual attention to all nine pastors. Now CCC is organized into two regions, and all the campus pastors answer to one of two regional pastors, both of whom in turn answer to Dave. Dave is now quite good at handling two people in the room with him!

Seacoast has a similar arrangement with our three regional pastors. As with CCC, all of our regional pastors are also campus pastors. LifeChurch.tv is also arranged by regions, but their regional pastors do not have dual roles.

At Seacoast, to keep the campus pastors connected to Greg Surratt, our senior pastor, and to help him experience the heartbeat of the campuses, we all share a meal together once a month. There is seldom a formal agenda other than Greg sharing what is on his heart. This is usually followed by an open forum for the campus pastors to ask anything they want. This free-for-all has helped us maintain a one-church environment rather than become a group of people who simply share a common name.

How Do You Answer the Money Question?

The final big structure question that most churches must consider is, how will they handle the money? Is it all put into one big pot, or does it get budgeted according to income? And who sets the budgets?

Originally, we set up our budgets at Seacoast on a 10/10/80 plan. Every campus budget was based entirely on how much money came in through the offerings at that campus. Ten percent of everything received went toward paying back the money spent to start the campus, 10 percent of the offerings went toward paying for central support, and 80 percent went toward operating the campus. The campus pastor was responsible for creating the budget for the 80 percent that stayed at his campus, even though all the money went through one bank account.

We ran into a few problems with this arrangement. First, the campuses felt as though Seacoast were more of a bank than a family. They disliked the idea of paying back a loan. Some jokingly wondered what would happen when they finished paying the loan. Were they then free to join the Mormons? It all seemed too formal and contractual.

A second challenge was the 10 percent budgeted for central support. While 10 percent was a good round number, it didn't come anywhere close to paying for the expenses incurred by central support. The reality was that the newer campuses, which all happened to be smaller than the original campus, chipped in 10 percent of their budget for central support, and the original campus usually chipped in 30 percent of its budget.

A third problem with our original plan was that campuses wanted to spend every dime of the 80 percent left in their budget. This left virtually no money for local emergencies, catastrophes like Hurricane Katrina and the Asian tsunami, or the possibility that the real estate market could go south and the stock market melt down as it did in the fall of 2008. We decided we needed a new plan.

Eventually we settled on a slight revision—the 70/20/10 plan. Campuses are now asked to operate on 70 percent of the offerings that come in. Twenty percent of the offerings go to central support, and 10 percent are held in reserve for new initiatives. Rather than having campuses pay back their start-up costs, we now raise those funds through special offerings and out of the 20 percent they pay toward central expenses. CCC has adopted a similar plan.

Bay Area Fellowship in Corpus Christi, Texas, recently went to a radical new financial model: every campus has its own bank account. Each campus pays their own bills, and they live off the offerings that come in on Sundays. Multi-site Pastor John Atkinson says he was skeptical at first, but the new plan is working very well. The campus pastors love the freedom, and the accounting is much simpler.

Essentially, there is no one right way to organize multi-site finances. Each church will have to examine different options before deciding on the model that best fits its structure and context.

Plan on Morphing

Whether you have two or three campuses or your vision is for a one-hundred-campus multi-site ministry, your structure needs to be regularly examined for effectiveness. The book of Acts offers plenty of illustrations, starting with the group of seven the apostles added in Acts 6:1–6, that demonstrate how the structure of a church needs adjustments as it grows and responds to new needs—and your congregation is certainly no exception!

> There is no one right way to organize multi-site finances.

Here are some final questions you might ask yourself or discuss with your staff as you consider the structure of your multi-site church:

1. Is our structure too complicated? If it takes three phone calls, two emails, and an act of Congress to order new coffee cups, it might be time to simplify the structure.
2. Is our structure too flat? Is it clear to whom staff and volunteers should go when they need an answer?
3. Are our campus pastors too removed from hearing and rehearing the vision of the church? Is each campus moving toward becoming a kingdom unto itself?
4. Do our leaders have enough freedom within our structure to lead?
5. Is our structure responsive to changing situations and needs?
6. Is our structure consistent with our vision?
7. Is our structure designed to accommodate growth?

Sometimes Less Is More

For most multi-site churches, which have two or three campuses, many different structures can work. In many ways, adding a second site is very similar to adding a new service, and it seldom necessitates going through a major overhaul of your leadership structure. It is wise, however, to continually be on the lookout for simpler ways to use your resources, both human and financial. Many multi-site churches have found that at least once a year they need to take a hard look at their structure and make sure they are still able to accommodate growth.

As you expand to multiple campuses, ask God to show you the people in your congregation who have the right gifts and know-how to morph and realign your structure so it fits each stage of need and growth.

As exciting as it can be when churches add additional sites, one of the most interesting developments in multi-site church growth is the opening of international campuses. For our next leg of the multi-site roadtrip, you'll need to grab your passport as we travel to Peru, India, and other far corners of the globe, visiting multi-site campuses around the world, starting just north of Seattle as our launching point.

CHRIST THE KING
COMMUNITY CHURCH
INTERNATIONAL

Mount Vernon, Washington

CHRIST THE KING COMMUNITY CHURCH INTERNATIONAL

FAST FACTS

Church vision ▶ *To see a prevailing, multi-location church emerge that will transform the spiritual landscape. This church will convene in thousands of small groups with worship centers strategically located in every community.*

Year founded ▶ *1999*

Original location ▶ *Mount Vernon, Washington*

Lead pastor ▶ *Dave Browning*

Teaching model for off-sites ▶ *Live teaching*

Denomination ▶ *Nondenominational*

Year went multi-site ▶ *2000*

Number of campuses ▶ *17 US; 100+ international*

Number of weekly services ▶ *23 US; unknown international*

Worship attendance (all physical sites) ▶ *4,000 US; 10,000 international*

Largest room's seating capacity ▶ *600*

Internet campus? ▶ *No*

International campus? ▶ *Yes*

Internet address ▶ *www.ctkonline.com*

In the business arena, people such as the Austrian celebrity chef Wolfgang Puck have opened up fine-dining restaurants and catering services all over the world. Across the globe, Puck has uncovered many locations where people enjoy his particular style of food.

Are there parallels with the spiritual food we offer through the church? The message of the gospel can be spread globally through internet-posted sermons, iPod downloads, CDs, church-sent missionaries, and church members whose work takes them overseas.

But something new is happening. The technology and mentality now exists for a church to have a campus in another country thousands of miles away, and many churches are developing a stronger level of ministry partnership in the process.

I (Warren) vividly remember my sense of surprise when I visited Christ the King Community Church International, where Dave Browning serves as senior pastor. Christ the King is based just north of Seattle, in a mildly run-down, single-story building that has the feel of a converted Elks lodge. Microsoft's headquarters are also in the area, and as I walked from my car to this global spiritual facility, I thought of the interesting parallels between the worldwide reach of that corporation and the multinational influence of the church I was about to visit.

When I arrived, Dave gave me a tour of all the rooms in the building (it was a short tour), beaming with excitement about the many ways in which God is going to use this church to impact the world. Greater Seattle is only a small part of that larger dream. Dave has a vision to replicate small groups and worship centers all around the world. Geographic limitations are irrelevant to his model. Dave's passion is simply to see lives changed by Jesus Christ, largely through neighborhood-based small groups and corporate worship centers, each led by someone local to the neighborhood, trained online by Christ the King Church.

Christ the King held its first worship service in 1999. Although the initial growth was impressive and led the limited-facility congregation to expand to three services within a year, Dave's greatest excitement was the start of thirty-eight small groups by the end of the first year. Each week, groups were convening in Jesus' name for Bible discussion, prayer, friendship, support, and encouragement. Some of these small groups eventually led to the start of new worship centers in nearby towns, with two centers launching in 2000, one the following year, another the year after that, and two more in 2004. In just four years Christ the King became a multi-location church with a sizable number of people who had never been to the original facility in Mount Vernon, Washington. All a church member needed was a small group and a local teacher, and Dave's heart was to train that local teacher to minister to that local group.

As people began showing some interest in developing small groups and worship centers, Dave started Christ the King University, an online, multimedia approach to leadership development. In just a short time Christ the King Community Church International began living up to their name as they spread regionally, crossed state lines, and expanded to other countries. All of this, growing out of a simple dream to see a church with thousands of small groups and worship centers, one strategically located in every community, placed in towns both locally and around the world!

Christ the King's international campuses are connected more through a partnership of values than through the week-to-week teaching. Its Nepal campuses are legally registered as Christ the King Relief and Development Services. The campuses worship God, are able to do good works in their communities, and are legally able to receive donations from outside the country. They translate that funding into physical expressions (food, clothing, etc.) of Christ's love. In South Africa, Christ the King exists mainly in the form of cell groups. Over seven hundred small groups, representing about eight thousand people, meet regularly. Most of the church life in South Africa currently occurs through these cells rather than through large worship centers.

Christ the King's international leaders gather annually, in person at its original location in Mount Vernon, for a time of fellowship and planning. Throughout the year, they remain in regular contact with the original campus and one another through email, the church's website, and phone calls.

Visiting an International Campus

Throughout this book, you've been reading the first-person accounts of site visits we've made. You've heard all about the amazing restaurants Geoff, Greg, and I were able to go to during our stateside visits. And you might be wondering which of us was able to score a globetrotting tour of the Christ the King campuses, to see them live and in action.

Unfortunately, none of us has that kind of funding. So we tried the next best thing—using someone else's money! The *Wall Street Journal* had phoned me, asking for some advice on a story they were developing about U.S. multi-site churches with international campuses. I gave them a list of a half-dozen options—limiting it to the places I wanted to visit—and then offered to tag along. As you've probably guessed, they weren't too excited about that idea. I even mentioned Christ the King's international office near the Microsoft headquarters and how the church was involved in five different countries. No interest.

So I tried the *next* next best thing. I asked the churches themselves (not just Christ the King), "How do you work with your overseas campus pastors? How much does it cost you to do supervision and coaching for a campus that's thousands of miles away? Would you like to send me somewhere to observe and report on it?"

In talking with the churches, I learned an important lesson about working internationally today. Most of the churches had found simple and very inexpensive alternatives to the high cost of frequent international travel. Dave Browning invited me in on several conversations with campus pastors in Nepal and South Africa. Another multi-site church involved me with its campuses in the Philippines and Australia. A third church let me join their weekly staff meeting, which included their campus pastor in Peru (I'll describe that in a minute).

But for each of these experiences, I didn't go to an airport. Nor did I taste any exotic food. In fact, I didn't even leave my house! With my computer, a telephone, a high-speed internet connection, and a twenty-five-dollar webcam, I was able to connect with campus pastors on almost any continent.

Skyping into the Campus Pastor Meeting

My experience with Flamingo Road Church (introduced in chapter 6), a Southern Baptist congregation based in south Florida, was fairly typical of the cost-effective way in which multi-site churches are staying connected internationally. As you may recall, Flamingo Road has seven campuses: five surrounding Fort Lauderdale (four in English, one in Spanish), one internet campus, and one campus in Lima, Peru. When I asked how the campuses stayed in contact with one another (including the Lima campus), Chris Brown, teaching pastor with a dual role as campus director, invited me to figuratively sit in on their next staff meeting.

A few minutes before the meeting began, I connected my webcam and logged in to my Skype account (free at www.skype.com). "Someday we're going to describe this experience as primitive technology and laugh about it," the church's tech director said as he explained what he was about to do next. "I want you to meet everyone here." To start off the meeting, he panned his webcam around the room, introducing each person physically present. Then he turned his webcam-mounted laptop computer away from himself toward another laptop, which was also equipped with a webcam. "We've Skyped Steve Guschov, our

Lima campus pastor, on this computer," he said. "Warren and Steve, I want you to meet each other."

It must have seemed pretty comical to the others in the room to watch two laptop computers face each other with two people on the computer screens interacting with one other. I was at my home in New York, Steve was at his house in Lima, and the laptops connecting us were in an office in Cooper City, Florida. The beauty of global connectivity—all without any long-distance or broadcast charges!

Steve and I didn't talk for very long, because we had already met by phone (I had interviewed him the week before this meeting). To reach him when he's in Peru, you simply dial the main church line, punch a certain extension, and the call is transferred over the internet to Peru (via Skype again) at virtually no extra cost. Our phone interview had been as simple and clear as it would've been had I called a church down the street from my house.

The tech director then repositioned the laptop computers so we could see some of the Florida-based team (he couldn't fit everyone into the camera angle). Steve and I could hear each other but not see each other anymore. Even though it required some simple, low-tech maneuvers—it worked! Several months after this meeting, the church began using TokBox, which eliminates the need to place laptops face-to-face or hang a mirror on the opposing wall.

Flamingo Road's International Campus

Once the weekly Thursday morning campus pastor meeting began, I found that it was remarkably similar to other staff meetings in multisite churches. In the case of Flamingo Road, all the campuses were using video for the main teaching at their services, so they debriefed last weekend's services, encouraged each other with the different ways in which they saw God at work, and discussed some of the technical challenges they needed to handle before the weekend. Senior Pastor Troy Gramling had just begun a new series that involved a door as a prop in his teaching. During the message, he would ask the people, "Will you step through the door and show love to those you meet, or will you stop at the door and not go through?" Stepping through the door had caused Troy to disappear from the camera at one point, and the campus pastors were hoping that this could be addressed before next week's broadcast. Troy's teaching had concluded with a call for people to come forward in response. While this had worked just fine at some of the campuses, it had created some problems at others. "If we do that again, we'll set up two stations for people to respond," said one of the campus pastors.

Throughout the call there was plenty of laughter, teasing, and bantering back and forth. I got the feeling that this was a team, that none of the campus pastors felt isolated or alone. Their conversations and interaction demonstrated a clear sense of unity and an understanding that they were part of something bigger than their individual campuses. I could sense that they also felt supported and connected, and they appreciated having an advocate in Chris Brown as he spoke with other Flamingo Road staff on their behalf. (In addition to the campus pastor meeting, all of those gathered, including Peru's Steve Guschov via Skype, are part of an all-staff meeting on Tuesdays.)

I was struck by one inescapable fact as I attended the Flamingo Road staff meeting: it didn't matter whether the campus was fifteen miles away or fifteen hundred miles away; each campus pastor understood his role of adapting the Flamingo Road experience to his congregation's unique size, culture, and context.

But I wanted to probe even further into the international campus. How did this actually work for the pastor in Lima, given the significant cultural and linguistic differences? Steve Guschov is an American, a lawyer from Boston who developed a heart for Lima while traveling there with a Bible distribution group. He married a Peruvian woman—the daughter of a pastor—and in 2005 sensed (and initially fought) a strong calling from God to launch a church designed to reach the growing class of Peruvians who speak English. At that point he didn't know anything about Flamingo Road. His non-denominational congregation was the first English-speaking church in Lima. During the first year of the church, they grew from three people—Steve, his wife, Dorcas, and her brother Christian—to over one hundred. About half of the congregation were Peruvians, and the rest were internationals, including a handful of Americans. Many of the people had come with a desire to practice English, and they ended up meeting Jesus in the process.

Meanwhile, back in the United States, Flamingo Road had been sending mission teams to Lima since 1994 and had gotten to know Steve's father-in-law, a local pastor in Lima. Troy Gramling and another senior staff member came to Lima on one of the mission trips in 2005 and, in conversation with Steve, came up with the novel idea of turning the new church into a campus of Flamingo Road.

> Many of the people had come with a desire to practice English, and they ended up meeting Jesus in the process.

"They approached us because our family already had a relationship with Flamingo Road," Steve explains. "The partnership gave us opportunity to do more than we were doing, sort of like catching a train already moving down the tracks." Flamingo Road wanted to partner with the new church in their social projects and offered financial support of Steve's mission church until it became self-sufficient.

Balance between American and Indigenous

Steve is insistent on making sure the church, including his own leadership, is as indigenous to Peru as possible. "I'm making every effort to learn the native language and embrace the local culture," he says. "It will pay off big-time, we are certain." He likes to draw an analogy between the McDonald's hamburger chain in southern Florida and the McDonald's outlets in Lima. The restaurants look and smell pretty much the same. The Big Macs and Quarter Pounders even taste the same, as do the fries. But at the fifteen to twenty McDonald's restaurants in downtown Lima, you can also order fried yucca, a local favorite, and fried chicken, since Peruvians typically prefer chicken over beef. You can order yourself an Inca Kola, the number one soda in Peru. At breakfast time, in addition to your regular Egg McMuffins, you can order breakfast sandwiches made with Peruvian country ham and garnished with onion salad.

"That's what successful international ministry is all about," he summarizes. "International ministry is about taking the best of what you have to offer, and adding to it that which is appealing to the local population. Then you have a combo that works!"

For Steve, that combo includes an English-language point of interest. His best advertising responses come from the city's top rock-and-roll radio station. "It's Spanish, but the vast majority of the songs are English-language," Steve explains. The church's top referrals come from schoolteachers who teach English. "If you want some good practice, go to this church," they tell their students.

> "International ministry is about taking the best of what you have to offer, and adding to it that which is appealing to the local population."

Even though English is the second language for most people who attend Flamingo Road Lima, and much of the ministry is done in Spanish, the church still conducts some of its ministry in English. When the American embassy began looking around for a nongovernmental organization that might offer care to the nineteen Americans in Peruvian prisons (most on drug charges), Flamingo Road Lima stepped up to the challenge. They provided toiletries, clothing, and Bibles as reading materials. They're trying to schedule regular visits as well. "Most of these people have been abandoned by their families. They have nothing, and some of the local jails make American prisons look like the Four Seasons Hotel," Steve says. This outreach also gives the church a relational bridge to the people who work at the American embassy.

The church has a number of Spanish-language outreaches as well, and has even planted a daughter church in the Amazon jungle, among the Yagua tribe.

The transition to joining the Southern Baptists and becoming a campus of Flamingo Road occurred in 2006. By 2008 the church was seeing an attendance of four hundred people in two services, one in English and a second in Spanish. Attendance at the English service is double the Spanish service attendance. During the church's 2007–2008 reporting year, it conducted fifty-seven baptisms.

Forget FedEx's Overnight Promise for Peru

As we discussed in chapter 7, there are many options for doing video teaching, any of which can become complicated! Getting the video messages to Peru took Flamingo Road a while to figure out. At first the church would FedEx a DVD to Steve, hoping he could run it the following Sunday, but even overnight packages in Peru can take weeks to clear customs. To ease the stress that comes from waiting for the mail, most services at the Lima campus are now two weeks behind the live messages at the Cooper City campus in south Florida.

Flamingo Road Lima also wanted to provide transcripts of the messages in both English and Spanish. The existing Spanish translations, which work well for Flamingo Road's Spanish-language campus in Florida, needed further translation and contextualization for Peru. For example, if the teaching pastor mentions Wal-Mart in his message, all Floridians — both English and Spanish speakers — know what that is, but for the Peruvian version, Wal-Mart needed to be replaced with the name of a large department store in Lima. Similarly, the subtitles on the videos needed to be adjusted for Peruvian culture and the Peruvian nuances of Spanish.

It's not unusual for worshipers at Flamingo Road Lima to pick up the printed transcripts, both English and Spanish, as they follow along, even if all they need help with is an occasional slang phrase. "Many of our worshipers are young people who are learning English," says Steve, "and so every Sunday morning they receive a double blessing: they get to practice their English at church, and they also get to hear God's Word taught in a contemporary and impactful manner."

Humorously, the question Steve and the church's first-impressions team are asked the most is not about the use of video teaching. Rather it's about the location of Flamingo Road, since Lima has no such street. "We're happy to field it, because it's more of a good conversation starter than a stumbling block," he says.

Other Models for International Campuses

If you pay a visit to the website www.thebridgecc.org or look at the printed literature of The Bridge Community Church, Decatur, Indiana, you are sure to see this slogan: "One dynamic church. Four diverse locations." Three of those locations are found in the small to medium-size towns of northwest and central Indiana. But the fourth location is truly diverse, and it is located 7,800 miles away. A few clicks at the website, and pictures appear with this caption: "Our first new church opened outside of the United States in the fall of 2005 in Bihar, India, under the leadership of Pastor E. A. Abraham. The pictures ... were taken on the first Sunday where 475 people attended the service. Many people committed their lives to Christ and forty-eight were baptized. God is awesome!"

This Indiana church takes seriously its mission to "help people find their way back to God"—wherever they are living! But The Bridge Community Church uses a different model than does Flamingo Road in setting up an international campus. Whereas Flamingo Road's Lima campus is an intentional extension of the teaching and program emphases of the Cooper City campus, the India campus of The Bridge Community Church is more of a partnership.

"We stretch the idea by calling it a campus," admits Mo Hodge, lead teacher of The Bridge Community Church. One of the church's lay leaders is on the board of a missionary organization. Through it he got to know Pastor Abraham and commended a potential partnership to Mo. "Basically, we plugged in with a man whom God has used in an incredible way," Mo says. "Pastor Abraham has planted fifty churches in his state. He has become one of our missionaries. We helped fund a new worship site, which he called The Bridge, but it was completely developed and administrated by Pastor Abraham. He comes over here once a year, and between visits we stay in contact by email. This gives us a great connection to God's work in that area."

There are no parallels with sermon content or teaching themes between The Bridge Community Church and its India campus, but the two share the same name and doctrinal beliefs. The personal relationships and ongoing financial assistance also create a strong sense of partnership. "We hope to fund more campuses in India for Pastor Abraham, which he'll also call The Bridge," says Mo.

In a similar way, El Rey Jesus (King Jesus), one of America's largest Spanish-language churches, takes more of a partnership approach to its multi-site campuses, both nationally and internationally. Under the leadership of Guillermo Maldonado, the church's influence has extended far beyond its Miami-area base, an extension accelerated by its use of television broadcasts across Latin America. According to John Laffitte, executive vice president of the church's King Jesus Leadership Institute, El Rey Jesus supports three types of churches, the second and third of which have international implications:

1. *Daughter churches* are led by ministers who have been part of the original Miami-area campus. At the initiative of El Rey Jesus, these pastors are each sent out locally to open a new church, which eventually becomes separate and self-supporting, though allied to El Rey Jesus in spiritual kinship.

2. *Affiliated churches* are ones that have asked to have a spiritual covering of El Rey Jesus. Many of them are international. After appropriate screening as to whether a partnership is suitable, El Rey Jesus teaches the pastors, trains them, and provides them with materials. They remain the pastors of their churches. El Rey Jesus also brings them to south Florida annually for teaching, training, and fellowship.

3. *Satellite churches* are those congregations who are watching the El Rey Jesus services as part of their worship. El Rey Jesus sends each one an "overseer" who functions as a campus pastor—the person on the ground during the service time. Some watch the entire service, while others use their own praise and worship band and watch only the teaching. Some receive the signal through the internet (low bandwidth) and

others by satellite (high-quality). For these churches, Pastor Maldonado is seen as their pastor.

Common Themes in International Campuses

In our interviews with churches that have opened international campuses, several themes became apparent:

- ▶ *Technology.* All of the arrangements we looked at depended on technology to stay connected. This included regular communication between the leadership, air travel back and forth, and where applicable, the regular exchange of teaching content. All of the relationships have some form of ongoing communication, whether by email, by phone, or in person. A majority of the churches connect face-to-face at least once a year.

- ▶ *Initiative.* Most international campus arrangements are initiated by an overseas party, rather than by an American church looking to replicate itself in another culture. Sometimes it can occur through a peer-level discussion. Either way, most international campuses are started through a personal connection, where someone knows someone and begins the conversation based on a preexisting relationship.

- ▶ *Common language.* Many of the international multi-sites have their services in English and do most of their back-and-forth communication in English. If another language is involved, the American church typically has some kind of history with that tongue.

- ▶ *Control.* The level of control ranges widely from church to church. Some churches, like Flamingo Road in Lima, are true extensions of the sending church, though with appropriate cultural adaptation. Other churches partner at a broader level, where it doesn't matter that one congregation speaks primarily one language and the other speaks primarily another language.

- ▶ *Emphasis on life change.* Churches partner with other congregations thousands of miles away because they passionately believe they're able to help change lives. Peter Taylor, age fifty-one, is today a New Zealand campus pastor of Living Hope Church (introduced in chapter 12), which is based in Washington State. The New Zealand campus was birthed in early 2008. Previously Peter spent eleven years as an associate pastor at another New Zealand church, but after coming to the West Coast, interning at Living Hope for a month, and catching the vision of the church, he went back to New Zealand, accompanied by a short-term mission team from Living Hope, and started a new Living Hope campus.

"Living Hope caught my attention because of the way they were able to get the unchurched into their buildings, love them, and ultimately see them give their lives over to God," Peter explains. In the new campus's first nine months, it grew from twenty-five people to over one hundred. It also baptized twenty people, most of them recent converts. "We are seeing people who would not normally darken the door of a church check us out and then come back for months on end and then eventually, at least for many, yield their lives to God," says Peter.

According to Living Hope's lead pastor, John Bishop, reports like this are what justify the idea of a campus seven thousand miles away. "Peter had a heart to genuinely reach lost people. If our teaching and training can help him do so, then we want to be part of it."

More Partnerships Ahead

The international campus movement is likely to accelerate and spread throughout other churches. As recently as one hundred years ago, it would take a missionary several weeks — even months — to travel to the "far-flung fields," a journey limited to those with the health and physical stamina to make it. A century ago the only way to travel overseas was by steamship, and the final leg of the overall journey would often include travel by rail, by paddleboat, by horseback, or on foot. Communication was limited to handwritten letters, which could often take months in transit before reaching the intended recipient.

Today air, rail, and vehicle travel to those same far-flung cities can occur within one day, enabling teams of all ages and fitness levels to engage firsthand in different aspects of mission work. A mission team today can post their work on YouTube or a similar site before the end of the day to share what they are doing with those back home. Today's internet and phone connections, coupled with attached-file photos and hand-shot video clips, make communication instant, easy, and highly interactive. Junior — or Grandma — can leave town on Friday night, and the church can watch a video report and then pray together for the ministry on Sunday.

> International campuses are likely to increasingly expand to new and even more innovative models for partnership.

Today's church culture values a hands-on, relational approach to missions. It is also growing in its ability to make missions a two-way street, where both parties genuinely respect one another and have valuable contributions to make. International campuses are likely to increasingly expand to new and even more innovative models for partnership.

Taking Your Church Global

So what about *your* church? Do you have any international connections who have expressed an interest in developing an international campus? What would be the benefits, for you and those you partner with? What would be the challenges or liabilities?

We suspect that with each hands-on overseas mission experience your church encounters, you will continue to revisit this issue. The key is to remain open to God's guidance as you seek his direction for your church in overseas partnerships.

Meanwhile, it's time for us to be on our way again. The truth is that while some churches are expanding internationally, bringing their teaching into new settings, your church might be considering the opposite experience—inviting a church from somewhere else (overseas or domestic) to bring its teaching to you! It's sort of like having a frequent guest speaker but via digital transit rather than airline or car. To help you get a taste of what it's like to welcome a regular teaching partner into your church, we're going to pay a visit to Albany, New York. Fasten your seat belt as we hit the road!

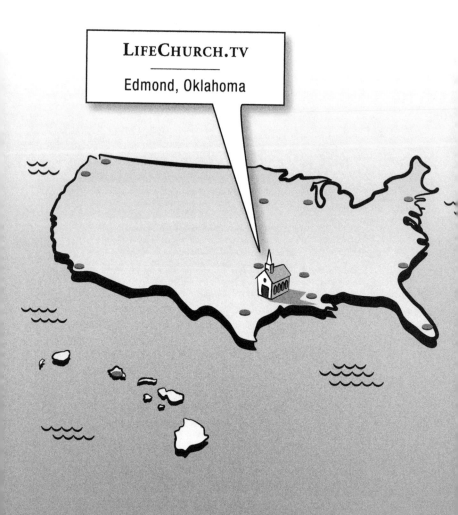

LIFECHURCH.TV

Edmond, Oklahoma

LIFECHURCH.TV

FAST FACTS

Church vision ▶	*To lead people to become fully devoted followers of Christ.*
Year founded ▶	*1996*
Original location ▶	*Edmond, Oklahoma*
Lead pastor ▶	*Craig Groeschel*
Teaching model for off-sites ▶	*Primarily video/DVD*
Denomination ▶	*Evangelical Covenant*
Year went multi-site ▶	*2001*
Number of campuses ▶	*14*
Number of weekly services ▶	*71*
Worship attendance (all physical sites) ▶	*26,462*
Largest room's seating capacity ▶	*1,800*
Internet campus? ▶	*Yes*
International campus? ▶	*No*
Internet address ▶	*www.lifechurch.tv*

For a growing number of churches, the primary teaching pastor is hundreds or thousands of miles away. This shift has big implications for the campus pastor and other local staff, in terms of the vision and local leadership roles.

I (Warren) have found that a great way to get the pulse of a church is to talk to as many people as I can bump into after a service. I've had some of my best, most informative conversations while chatting with people in a church hallway. On one of my roadtrip visits, I spent some time at the LifeChurch.tv campus in Albany, New York, asking people how they were dealing with the fact that their teaching pastor was located twelve hundred miles from their campus. I happened to run into Rob Carey, an uber-volunteer at the campus. I quickly observed that Rob and his wife, Karen, probably know the people, the history, the organization, and the heart of the Albany campus better than anyone else. So I figured he'd be a good person to ask.

"When you're inviting your friends or relatives to this church, what do you tell them?" I asked. He grinned and replied, "My biggest selling point is that it's only one hour long." And he was right about that! The service had run exactly one hour, to the minute. "That works for some people whose image of church is something that goes on and on and on," he explained.

After thinking more seriously about my question, though, Rob continued, "Mostly I tell them that our church is not what you'd normally expect. I talk about our great band, the way we use a fog machine and theater lights, the children's and youth program—how everything is different and they need to come with an open mind."

"Do you mention anything about the pastor being twelve hundred miles away?" I asked, referring to the fact that the teaching pastor, usually Craig Groeschel, is beamed live by satellite from Oklahoma.

"Craig's a strong speaker," he replied, "but I don't even mention what we do for teaching. Just getting them there is the point, and then it's God's part from there."

I chatted with several other people in the church lobby and asked them the same question: how did they feel having a teaching pastor so far away from their campus? For all the people I talked with, it was basically a nonissue. "Everything about this church is different, and a lot of people say they like it," was a common reply.

I've sat in on several LifeChurch.tv messages at churches around the country. Craig has great eye contact, and he makes a point of continually referring to the campuses as he talks, so I've always felt included when he preaches. Whether I was visiting a campus in New York, Florida, or Oklahoma, Craig always spoke in a way that seemed to fit the congregation. Most importantly, though, he was careful to take the timeless Word of God, apply it to his own life, and then challenge hearers like me to apply that Word in very relevant, practical, compelling ways. Visiting a LifeChurch.tv campus is no different in many ways from having a terrific guest speaker at my local church—it's always a blessing when God uses a gifted communicator to speak to my mind and heart.

Having a guest speaker in a local church is nothing new. And so it is not all that unusual to find that people are growing spiritually from a steady diet of out-of-town preaching, a reality made all the more frequent through the use of the internet, radio, and television.

What is new, however, is the idea of combining those two ideas together: getting my weekly teaching *at church* from someone I've never met who lives in another city or state—or perhaps country. How is it possible for a church to do all it needs to do, when the main teaching comes from someone who isn't even there?

The answer is simple: you can't do it alone. And Craig has plenty of help. That's where Josh Brower comes in. Josh is the campus pastor at LifeChurch.tv in Albany. Josh does everything *except* teach, providing a "face for the place" and giving primary leadership to the face-to-face outreach and discipleship of the Albany congregation.

The roles typically associated with a senior pastor have simply been divided between two people. Craig, as the lead pastor, is the primary Bible teacher. He also provides directional leadership to the LifeChurch. tv movement. Josh, as the campus pastor, personalizes the church and shepherds the flock. He spends most of his week training leaders, building relationships, and helping the Albany congregation reach out to new people while caring for one another.

WHAT MAKES A GREAT CAMPUS PASTOR?

As you might imagine, the role of the campus pastor is critical to the success of a model like this. But what makes for a really good campus pastor? My friend Jim Tomberlin, mentioned on pages 170, 181, and 219, publishes a free e-newsletter called *Multi-Sightings* through his Third Quarter Consulting group (www.ThirdQuarterConsulting.com). In one edition of his newsletter, Jim acknowledged the growing demand among churches for qualified people to serve as campus pastors:

Almost every week I receive a call from a church desperately searching for a campus pastor. We have come a long way from the early days of the multi-site movement when no one knew what a campus pastor was, or if they did, weren't interested in being one. Once seen as an emcee for a video service, the campus pastor role is becoming one of the most sought-after church staff positions in the Church.

Below I boil down my suggestions for what makes a great campus pastor. Assuming that this individual is a spiritually mature person of Christ-like character with a proven track record, an ideal campus pastor matches at least several of the points in this description.

1. Catalytic Leader: The campus pastor should be a high energy, self-starter who not only gets things done, but is able to make new things happen.
2. Multi-Tasker: A high-capacity player who is able to juggle a lot of balls simultaneously and love it.
3. People Magnet: A relational "animal" who draws people like flies to honey.

4. Team Player/Builder: Should not be a lone ranger, but is able to work within the system and turn followers into teams.
5. Communicator: The campus pastor doesn't have to be an exceptional Bible teacher, but is comfortable and articulate when speaking to a room full of people.
6. DNA Carrier: Should bleed the vision and default to the mission and values that align with the senior leadership of the church.

There are also some traits that are *not* conducive to a campus pastor:

1. A person who feels compelled to preach (unless you put them on the teaching team).
2. An independent-spirited entrepreneur.
3. Someone with an agenda other than reaching people far from God and growing a congregation.

So where do you find campus pastors? Often, it's best to start by looking internally, within your existing church. Who on your staff right now already has the DNA of your church? Is there someone who has proven to be faithful and is ready for a new challenge? Who are the best people on your team? Lead out with those people.

If you don't see a possibility on your existing church staff, then consider those who are in your congregation who might be able to transition into this role. There are many high-capacity individuals serving in the marketplace, sitting in your church who have the leadership capacity and are looking for a place to serve God in a new way.

The next best place to look is within the larger network of your own staff connections. Who are the people around the country that your staff thinks would be good campus pastor candidates? Consider bringing them on the team and giving them some time to grow and learn. Take a year to train them at your home base before launching them into their own campus.

Finally, you can put ads in places like the Willow Creek Exchange, ChurchStaffing.com, Tony Morgan's jobamatic blog, and the various denominational networks for hiring pastors.

Levels of Sharing a Communicator

LifeChurch.tv offers its shared communicator resources at three levels. The first level, called Open, represents the idea that any church anywhere can download any number of the free resources LifeChurch.tv posts on its http://open.lifechurch.tv/ website. The content on the site includes message series artwork, themed videos that can be used to promote and brand a series, message outlines, and layered graphic files. To use these resources, churches must agree to a license agreement stating that they will use the content only in a noncommercial manner in an effort to "lead people to become fully devoted followers of Christ." Churches in the Open level also agree to make no association by name to LifeChurch.tv or its resources.

In 2009 Lifechurch.tv took the Open concept to another level with the launch of VideoTeaching.com. They describe the site as an easy-access online library full of high-quality video messages from a variety of gifted Christian communicators. Some of the early contributors to the library include Francis Chan and Brian Houston, as well as Lifechurch.tv's senior leader, Craig Groeschel. As with all of Lifechurch.tv's offerings, VideoTeaching.com is a free resource.

A second level, known as Network, is for churches that want to use LifeChurch.tv video teaching messages in one or more of their weekly worship services. Again, all of the resources are free. Network churches maintain one hundred percent autonomy in all their areas of ministry, including the church leadership, vision, decision making, and governance, but they also use the tagline "a part of the LifeChurch.tv Network" in the promotion and delivery of the weekly message.

The third level, which includes Josh Brower and the Albany campus, is called United. Congregations in this level officially become LifeChurch.tv campuses, part of the core vision of being one church in multiple locations. United campuses become fully aligned, governed, and led by LifeChurch.tv leadership.

A Leadership Trio

LifeChurch.tv models well this concept of dividing the pastor and teacher roles between two people. Heartland Community Church in Rockford, Illinois, spreads them out between *three* people. From day one, one person, who came from the marketplace, has filled the role of directional leader. A second person, an ordained minister, has served as worship leader. A third person has been the teacher represented by the internal videotape library of Willow Creek Community Church in South Barrington, Illinois.

It all started back in 1998, when Mark Bankord approached Bill Hybels, pastor at Willow Creek, and asked him for permission to use videos of Willow teaching messages as part of a new church plant. "You're nuts," Bill replied. But Mark persisted, explaining his passion for getting the best teaching he knew out in front of his friends. He insisted that Bill's messages would work just as well in Rockford as they did in the Chicago area.

"Will anybody come?" Bill asked. Neither one of them really knew, but Mark was willing to take the risk. "I'm in if you're in," Bill said. "Let's give this six months and see what God is up to."

Mark was a marketplace leader, not a pastor, so he approached his friend and evangelism partner, Doug Thiesen, an ordained pastor and gifted worship leader, and shared his vision. They started the church together, and it turned out that the video approach worked! The church grew year after year, and today they have three campuses.

The strength of the video teaching model is that it often enables a release of the spiritual gift of leadership locally at the church. "Too often there's no on-ramp for strong leaders," Mark says. "Too many churches are full of untapped leaders." At Heartland, leaders are welcome to lead, teachers to teach, and pastors to pastor. "It's the ideal platform for high-capacity lay leaders," says Mark. "We have 130 staff today. Ten come with formal ministry training, but everyone else is from the marketplace."

In 2008 Heartland Community Church brought a full-time teaching pastor on-site, so outside video is not used nearly as much today, although some of the off-site campuses still use video teaching from the Rockford campus. "But even today with a teaching pastor on-site," says Mark, "people understand that I'm *leading* the church while he is doing the *teaching*."

Strategic Partnerships

At Connexus Community Church in Barrie, Ontario, about fifty miles north of Toronto. Pastor Carey Nieuwhof has a track record as an effective teacher and leader. In 2007 he resigned from an existing church in Barrie and started Connexus on the other side of town. To be entirely accurate, we should say that he started a church with *two* campuses, one in Barrie and another one twenty miles away in Orillia. Both campuses meet in movie theaters at 8:30 and 10:00 a.m., and both have grown quite rapidly. (Then in 2009 they launched a third campus.) Though a number of people attending come from churches where Carey previously served as a pastor, the total attendance at the church hit about six hundred by the one-year mark, a phenomenal number for a Canadian church.

Carey serves as the teaching pastor at Connexus about seventy-five percent of the time, teaching in person at one campus and via video at the other campus. The other twenty-five percent of the time, his most frequent teaching staff is Andy Stanley—via video.

"Andy's been one of my favorite preachers, influencing me heavily," Carey explains. "I had heard him at a leadership conference and then began buying his books and downloading his sermons."

Carey had followed Andy Stanley for seven years before he started Connexus. As he was planning the new church, Carey had talked with North Point Community Church in Alpharetta, Georgia, about adding Andy as a regular teaching pastor via video. They said yes.

I asked Carey, Why not look locally instead? "I am looking to develop a local communicator as an additional teacher, but I don't have that kind of person at present," Carey told me. "Andy's teaching raises the quality bar for us. I brought in Andy's teaching because he's more gifted than I am as the prime communicator. I think people can have an appetite for up to three regular communicators: primary, secondary, and occasional guest."

This arrangement is made possible through what North Point calls strategic partnerships. These are churches across North America that share with North Point the same mission, values, beliefs, and strategy. Often, as North Point is involved in conversations with another healthy growing church, the question arises, "Could we go farther faster for God's kingdom by working together?" It's usually a discussion triggered by a desire for greater, strategic influence.

How does Carey handle the cultural differences between two countries, not to mention two different spiritual and geographic climates? He finds it readily manageable. He may not make as much use of a teaching series like *Letters to the President*, or a series with major references to a U.S. hockey team. "The translation factor is nearly ninety percent workable in our culture," he says, "since both countries listen to the same music and watch the same movies and television shows."

Perhaps a more typical example of a strategic partner church is found in the small town of Dothan, Alabama, some 250 miles southwest of North Point's base campus. In 1995 Andy Stanley and a group of five other leaders began North Point Community Church in Alpharetta, which is part of the Greater Atlanta area. As the church grew, it added a second worship center adjacent to its original worship center. This second venue required them to explore the use of video teaching at one of the auditoriums. As North Point continued to grow, it launched additional campuses twenty miles to the south and north. Both campuses primarily used video for the Sunday service teaching element.

Troy Fountain, who was a staff member at North Point during these launches, began to wonder: if the teaching could effectively be exported two hundred feet away (to the second auditorium) and also twenty miles away, then why not two hundred miles? God began leading Troy and his family to consider a move to Dothan to start what would later become North Point's first strategic partnership church.

Wiregrass Church held its first service in 2004 at a hotel in

Dothan. Almost all the teaching came through video. Since that time, the church has continued to grow, with Andy serving as a teaching pastor and Troy serving as the lead pastor (functionally equivalent to a campus pastor role). Troy leads the staff of Wiregrass Church in its day-to-day operations and in discerning the ministry needs of those who attend Wiregrass and live in the surrounding community.

Strategic partners such as Connexus and Wiregrass are different from North Point campuses in that each strategic partner is independently governed and financed, even though North Point supplies a helping hand in the early stages. All have a similar mission—to lead people into a growing relationship with Jesus Christ. All share the same beliefs and ministry values. All strategic partners use a similar foyer-to-kitchen strategy in which people move from being welcome guests to becoming family members in authentic community. All tap into the same resources available from North Point, from regular teaching content to innovative children's curriculum.

In addition, the lead pastors at all of the strategic partner churches, which numbered more than twenty by early 2009, communicate regularly with North Point's strategic partner director, and they attend a lead pastor annual retreat as well. Their teams, both key volunteers and staff, come twice a year to a mini-conference called n*rich.

Should You Bring In an Outside Teacher?

Churches that opt for a shared communicator—a teacher by video from another church—do so for lots of different reasons. The Albany campus of LifeChurch.tv follows a model of dividing the traditional pastor role between two people: teacher and campus leader. Heartland Church was motivated by a similar need in their decision to split the role into three people: directional leader, worship leader, and off-site video teacher. North Point's strategic partnerships are designed to enable high-potential churches to reach even farther by utilizing a proven teacher as the primary communicator and bringing in another person to serve as the local leader. Each of these models seeks to find the best possible people to serve in the proper roles, even if they aren't physically present.

There is yet another option we have not discussed yet—the possibility of a church merger. In the next chapter, we'll take a more in-depth look at churches that have utilized mergers as a way of stewarding their resources for maximum kingdom benefit. To get a taste of what it's like when churches merge together, we'll need to go to Long Island, New York. So start practicing your best New York dialect (say lawn-*guy*-land) and pray that we can avoid New York City's legendary traffic snarls!

SHELTER ROCK
CHURCH

Manhasset, New York

SHELTER ROCK CHURCH

FAST FACTS

Church vision ▶ **To lead as many people as possible into a joyful and growing relationship with Jesus Christ. To reach Long Island with the gospel of Jesus Christ through the continued development of multi-campus communities pursuing excellence in a culturally and age appropriate context and by working with other life-giving churches and Christian organizations toward this end.**

Year founded ▶ **1943**

Original location ▶ **Manhasset, New York**

Lead pastor ▶ **Steve Tomlinson**

Teaching model for off-sites ▶ **In-person teaching pastor**

Denomination ▶ **Conservative Baptist**

Year went multi-site ▶ **2005**

Number of campuses ▶ **2**

Number of weekly services ▶ **4**

Worship attendance (all physical sites) ▶ **900**

Largest room's seating capacity ▶ **400**

Internet campus? ▶ **No**

International campus? ▶ **No**

Internet address ▶ **www.shelterrockchurch.com**

After experiencing their first merger, some churches embrace the idea of pursuing additional, more intentional mergers, often called restarts.

Conventional wisdom will tell you that merging two churches together is usually a bad idea. Church growth consultant Lyle Schaller has said, looking back at the dismal fruit of the 1950s and '60s, when mergers were all the rage with denominational leaders, that "in too many mergers, the result was 4 plus 4 equals 6" — meaning a net decline in attendance and growth.[12]

Schaller was certainly right about one thing: it usually doesn't work when two declining churches join together. But what about a merger of a growing church with a struggling church? As I (Warren) have visited and studied some of the "merger campuses" of multi-site congregations, I've observed more of an acquisitions approach toward mergers. This new model is quite different from the older model that joined failing churches together. Early indicators even suggest that church mergers — in this new sense of completely restarting one of them — may hold significant potential for the future health and expansion of the American church.

Approach 1: Declining Restarts

Back in 1975 First Baptist Church in Manhasset, New York, was down to about fifteen people. The church had been founded some thirty years earlier as an outreach to soldiers coming home from World War II who were moving into this new section of Long Island. Gradually the flow of GIs stopped, the town became settled, and the congregation developed a wariness of "strangers" becoming part of their fellowship. That's usually not a hopeful sign for the future of a church!

That year, however, a new pastor began leading the church on a remarkable turnaround. He introduced some changes into the culture of the church so that its members were more welcoming to visitors. Subsequent pastors continued the growth, and by the time of my visit in 2008, attendance at the quarter-acre campus had grown to about five hundred adults and children. The church had two services, a packed 250-seat sanctuary, a 50-seat video venue, and various children's classrooms. They had renamed the church Shelter Rock Church in 2004, even while retaining their affiliation with the Conservative Baptist denomination.

The current pastor, Steve Tomlinson, is acutely aware of the turnaround that began in 1975. "I tell that story all the time because it shows what can happen when you take a difficult step for the greater cause of God's kingdom," he says. He shares the church's history with new members and fellow pastors to encourage a hope-filled faith in what God can do.

One pastoral acquaintance of Steve's was really discouraged. His church, about twenty minutes away, was experiencing major decline. Steve told him, "If you reach a point of throwing in the towel, please tell us." Eventually that's exactly what this minister did; he called Steve, asking for help. After several conversations between the pastors and with leaders of their respective congregations, they defined exactly what it might mean to merge the declining church into Shelter Rock.

It was important that Shelter Rock Church be the first to vote. "We did our vote first so that when the other congregation voted, they would have arms to fold into," Steve said. Then it was time for the other congregation to vote. The congregation knew they would be starting over. "We had made it clear that we wanted a total surrender," explained Steve.

The vote was conclusive: thirty yes, four no. A pastor from the church's glory days came back for the changeover, with a powerful message that "God is doing a new thing." The aging church building received some needed remodeling, as no money had been spent on it in years. Shelter Rock's teaching staff and musicians began leading the congregation, which had an immediate jump in attendance. And the church, which also belonged to the Conservative Baptist denomination, changed its name to Shelter Rock Church, Syosset campus.

That transition occurred in 2005. When I visited in 2008, attendance at this once dying church campus was now 260 adults and children meeting in two services. About one-third of the people had transferred from the Manhasset campus, one-third were former members of the old church who had been drawn back by the new start, and the remaining third were newcomers from the surrounding community.

The campus teaching pastor, Jack Crabtree, was particularly excited about some of the former members who had returned, enthusiastic about the change. Some had shared with him, "We always prayed that our church would be revived and filled again, but we never thought it would happen at this pace." One former member reported that another old-time member had come up to her in tears, saying, "I had to sit on the balcony." She had responded, "What is so bad about that?" and the woman had said, "You don't understand. I had to sit on the balcony—these are tears of joy."

It's stories like these that have inspired Shelter Rock in their two-campus approach. "Having the resources of the Manhasset church, both staff and generous financial help, has really moved things along here," Jack told me. He likes the friendly attitude between the campuses. "Everybody comes together and talks about what's best for everybody," he says.

Shelter Rock Church is currently one church on two campuses, but it may not be that way for long. Other churches with declining membership have approached Shelter Rock to begin a similar discussion. "My dream for what God might do is far beyond my ability," Steve says. "I think a lot of churches are looking for a way to get a fresh start on reaching their communities."

Approach 2: Healthier Restarts

If the first approach focuses on merging a declining church into a healthy church, what happens when you merge two churches that are both healthy? Or what about churches that have begun a turnaround and need some extra help as they seek to build momentum? Can merging help them accelerate their impact?

That's what we found as we looked at several of the mergers that have since become campuses of LifeChurch.tv (introduced in chapters 6 and 10). "We always ask, 'Can we do more together than apart?' and the answer must be yes," says Bobby Gruenewald, a member of the leadership team at LifeChurch.tv. "We want one plus one to equal five! That's when God is at work in a way where we want to be part of it."

The church's first merger experience was with a stable, older church located just a few miles from LifeChurch.tv's original campus. The pastor had been retiring, and the congregation had asked lead pastor Craig Groeschel to leave LifeChurch.tv to become their pastor. He responded, "Why don't *you* join *us*?" So that's what they did. Admittedly, it was an awkward and painful transition as the older church learned to embrace LifeChurch.tv's vision and ministry approach. The changes involved renaming the church, renaming the building, replacing the choir with a band, reducing the oversized staff, dissolving the church board, and more — taking on every sacred cow in the church. The lesson from the experience, according to Bobby? "We learned that God had additional mergers for us," he says. Today that campus draws thirty-five hundred to four thousand people weekly.

The second merger for LifeChurch.tv was a restart. A church in Fort Worth, Texas, had peaked at seven hundred to eight hundred several years previously, and then had dwindled to one hundred. The former youth pastor had been asked to return as the senior pastor. The church was selling their building and going portable, as part of a relaunch strategy. They approached LifeChurch.tv about a possible merger to give them a boost on their restart. Today that LifeChurch.tv campus draws seven hundred to eight hundred people weekly. In the first six months after the doors were opened, more than fifty people committed their lives to Christ.

The third merger was a restart, but of a healthy church. In Hendersonville, Tennessee, a Bible study had become a church, growing to about eighty people. At that point the small church decided they needed a larger track to run on. They were filled with vision and found they were a close match to the culture of LifeChurch.tv. The church's leaders approached LifeChurch.tv about merging, and in a record two months they became a LifeChurch.tv campus. At the one-year mark, the campus pastor said of the merger, "Every single week we've met, we've seen people come to Christ, and as a church we've grown more than seven hundred percent."

The fourth merger for LifeChurch.tv involved a church that was growing slowly but was located in a fast-growing area of Florida. "The pastor felt that being part of a bigger whole would help him reach more people in south Florida," Bobby explained. They too merged with LifeChurch.tv and have grown significantly.

The fifth merger involved another restart, this one in Albany, New York (highlighted in the previous chapter). A long-term pastor had built a strong church, but in the decade before his retirement the church had steadily declined. The congregation called a young pastor and blessed his ideas of renaming the church and making the worship more contemporary, all in an effort to reach new people and see future growth. The new pastor suggested that the church become a campus of LifeChurch.tv, and after much prayer and discussion the merger took place. In its first year as a LifeChurch.tv campus, it grew from eighty people to almost three hundred, baptizing over fifty—more than had been baptized in the previous decade.

Merger Decisions and Options

Bobby Gruenewald summarizes LifeChurch.tv's merger approach with the four Ds for a successful church merger:

- ▶ *Decision.* Both churches must discern: Is this what God has for us? Is this how God is leading us as a church?
- ▶ *Disruption.* It is critical that the change in the merging-in church's culture happens immediately, with a clear break in the culture, such as repainting the walls or inserting a new teaching pastor.
- ▶ *Development.* The emphasis here is on building the church,

very intentionally—from children's ministry to youth ministry to training adults in ministry.

▶ *Debut.* The launch weekend will be more an acknowledgment and celebration of what has already changed, as the church now goes public in reaching out to the community and making disciples.

When a church merges with LifeChurch.tv, it does far more than take on a name, such as LifeChurch.tv, Albany campus. It adopts the leadership, weekly teaching (live by satellite), children's programming, logo, and overall ministry approach. It truly becomes part of the LifeChurch.tv family, down to participating in the same missions projects. The campus leadership receives constant training and coaching and weekly feedback. LifeChurch.tv is one church in many diverse locations, but the campuses share one vision, one leadership team, one board, and one budget.

LifeChurch.tv uses the name United to describe the partnership level in which a church becomes a LifeChurch.tv campus. This was introduced in the previous chapter, along with two other partnership levels of accessing LifeChurch.tv's teaching. Only the United level involves mergers, however. As we saw in the previous chapter, only those churches willing to become part of the United network are accepted for the merger-restart process.

Not Neat and Clean

Churches with a track record of serial mergers affirm that the process of "mergering" is neither uniform nor predictable. Following are some generalities:

▶ *Initiation.* Regardless of the specific details of the merger, there is usually some level of personal connection between the churches. Sometimes the pastors met each other at a conference and hit it off. Sometimes the connection is very weak, such as when a church sends an email starting with "You don't know us. We've been watching your services on

LIFECHURCH.TV'S ADVICE ON MERGER DISCUSSIONS

Craig Groeschel's blog *Swerve* (http://swerve.lifechurch.tv/2008/10/30/the-public-merger-meeting/) explains how the LifeChurch.tv team approaches a merger discussion. Here is a lightly edited version of that entry:

Once everyone in leadership agrees that a unified effort is likely God's direction, you'll generally want to have at least one public meeting.

Assuming one church is taking the lead, the other church will likely want to gather to hear the vision and ask questions.

Here is how we've always done it: In each partnership we've entered, I've spoken to the partnering church and answered questions. Before the meeting, the other pastor (or leadership group) should have presented the idea to the people. Then we schedule a midweek evening event. Following worship, the pastor says something to the people, then introduces me.

After honoring the pastor, telling our story, and explaining what the partnership could look like, I always:

- *Explain that things will change drastically!* I never want people to believe it will be ministry as usual. If they don't want change, they shouldn't join us.
- *Explain how the leadership structure works.* We make sure everyone clearly understands how we function.
- *Describe how this has worked with other churches.* Because God has blessed each partnership we've entered to date, I always tell those stories.
- *Introduce the leaders of our church.* I want everyone to know our leaders, including one of our board members who was from a previous church we partnered with.
- *Cast a vision for reaching people.* The best reason to partner is to reach more people.
- *Answer questions.* People always want to know what will happen to their favorite ministry. I spend ample time honestly answering questions.
- *Allow people to vote.* We don't vote at our church, but I believe it is important for people who are giving up a lot to believe in their future. Every time we've done this, the people have voted overwhelmingly in favor of partnering.

the internet [or following your blog or using your resources], and we've been praying about whether ..."

▶ *First steps.* The church being invited to intervene tries to discern, "Is this something God wants us to do?" As one merger participant said, "We're talking about kingdom resources — both people and buildings — so the most important question is whether we could do more together than alone." Checklists for compatible chemistry include attitude toward reaching the lost, doctrine, financial status, and culture match between the congregations.

▶ *Speed.* For most mergers, things move very quickly in terms of a decision. There are numerous advantages to moving as rapidly as possible. Doing so will minimize the anxiety level of the congregation, maintain focus, and keep ahead of the rumor mill — word travels fast to neighbors and the local media! As one merger veteran commented, "The longer it takes, the more something can go wrong." In an informal Leadership Network poll, we found that the average window for most churches contemplating a merger was thirty to forty-five days from discussion to decision, even though the actual merger process often takes much longer as the decision is implemented.

▶ *Legal angle.* Churches with experience in mergers affirm that you need careful legal advice, and it's better to get it as early in the process as possible. You should try to get the church constitution and bylaws into an attorney's hand as soon as you can so a comparison can be made, lest everyone later have to vote again because of some legal loophole they skipped, or find they've unintentionally done something illegal. Find an attorney who can explain everything involved in legally transferring assets. You may discover that there are some surprises — even to the church being consolidated! ("We forgot that we own some mountain property that we sometimes use for youth retreats.") Translate the key differences into plain English for discussions. The process of merging might also include a nonbinding letter of intent, which gives participating churches some additional legal protection.

▶ *Goals and success.* Few veterans of multiple mergers frame their metrics primarily in terms of increased attendance or finances. Instead they figure out creative ways to measure the more intangible fruit of ministry. You might want to ask, for example, "Is the result a healthier environment for growth?" or "Are we moving a greater percentage of people into service capacity?" or "Is the culture of each church now stronger and more aligned for mission?"

One church took a tiered approach to measuring financial progress: tier one involves simply meeting the expenses for the church that was merged; tier two adds the factor of sharing, with a portion of the offerings at the merged location being sent back to support the "central service" expenses at the sponsoring church; the third tier adds an additional factor of giving above and beyond expenses, with funds being used to further the cycle by assisting in the merger of additional congregations.

▶ *Staffing.* Existing staff are sometimes released or repositioned as part of the merger. This may require some frank discussions about finances as well: "You're way overpaid for the size and stage the church currently represents." Generally, people with strong leadership gifts are needed for the kind of transitions necessary. Flexibility in structure is essential, as the church structure must be size and stage appropriate.

▶ *General advice.* "Be more open and clear up front." "Be redemptive in everything you do." "Adapt and be flexible—no two mergers are alike."

Big Mergers Are Newsmakers but Are the Exception

While it's helpful to know that mergers have worked well when a high-profile church "acquires" another well-known church, it's important to remember that these types of mergers are the exception, not the norm. Large church mergers tend to make the headlines because of their visibility.

One example that drew a lot of media attention was the merger of two Phoenix-area congregations. In this case it was the smaller church — CitiChurch in Scottsdale, a congregation of fifteen hundred people and only seven years old — that made the initial offer of merger to Word of Grace in east Mesa, a church of four thousand that had been in existence for twenty-five years and had a large campus complex. And it was the CitiChurch pastor, Terry Crist, age forty-two, who became the senior pastor of the combined two-campus church, while fifty-eight-year-old Gary Kinnaman transitioned to the pastor-at-large with occasional preaching duties in the merged church.

As *Church Executive* magazine reported the story, Word of Grace had experienced a couple years of decline before Gary announced to a group of local ministers that he was looking for someone to succeed him. Terry Crist heard about it from one of the CitiChurch members and wondered if this might be a kingdom opportunity to expand the multi-site vision of their young congregation. Two weeks later Gary and Terry were having breakfast together when Gary startled Terry by saying, "I'm looking for someone like you to lead Word of Grace into the future, someone younger with a proven track record and a long-term commitment to the Valley. Do you know of anyone you might recommend?"

Terry responded, "I can do better than that. I might be interested myself." Gary shared that he hadn't realized that Terry would consider leaving CitiChurch. And he was right. Terry had no plans to leave. But he had another idea: "I wouldn't leave, but we would entertain the possibility of Word of Grace merging with us."

The churches faced a number of challenging contrasts — the different communication styles of the two pastors, the different worship styles, and a difference between the average age of their attenders (a median age of forty-eight at Word of Grace versus an average age of thirty-six at CitiChurch). But most of all, the life cycle of each church was radically different. The church in Scottsdale was young, dynamic, and vision driven, while the church in Mesa was older, somewhat static, and more policy driven.

After considerable prayer and discussion, the Word of Grace board voted unanimously to merge with CitiChurch and become one church in two locations, separated by eighteen miles. The name City of Grace was recommended for the merged entity by a young staff member after Terry Crist expressed his desire to honor the past while forming a new identity that would carry them into the future. Each weekend City of Grace holds seven worship experiences, with four on the Scottsdale campus and three on the Mesa campus. Each campus currently holds one video service; all others are live. Both campuses are growing numerically and spiritually, with another campus under development. The City of Grace vision is to serve a congregation of ten thousand people on seven campuses throughout the Valley of the Sun.[13]

Jim Tomberlin consulted with both churches during the merger. As Jim notes, "Mergers come in three types: adoption, absorption, or an acquisition. This was more of an adoption because both congregations brought a lot to the table which was integrated into a new entity. Just like a child that is adopted into a new family, the adopted congregation takes on a new name and way of doing things but also enhances the new family with its unique DNA."

Not the Keys but the Mission

New Life Community Church is a multi-site church in twelve locations across downtown Chicago. Many of those campuses are churches that have merged into New Life as restarts. The church's 2008 merger offers a touching model for the ultimate strength of a merger: the idea of redeeming space and history by changing leaders and creating a totally new chapter in a church's mission.

Bethel Evangelical Lutheran Church had been in the Humboldt Park community for 114 years. After a solid 80 years of stability and health, the church went through about 20 difficult years of struggle and decline, and nearly as many pastors during that time. Eventually they reached a point where both the congregation and the sponsoring denomination agreed it was time to close the church.

Through a series of relationships, Ralph Kirchenberg, the seventy-six-year-old president of the church board, came to know the leadership and ministry of New Life. He championed the idea, which the denomination blessed, of deeding the church building, the school, and the parsonage to New Life after the church had formally been dissolved.

On the day of the dissolution, some two hundred people gathered for the ceremony. It was an emotional time of memories, prayers, and a final Holy Communion for Bethel Evangelical Lutheran Church.

The printed program specified that at the end of the service, Ralph would give the keys to Mark Jobe, lead pastor of New Life Community Church. Both stood and Ralph began to speak. "It says in the program that we are to hand over the keys to New Life at this point," he said, "but you know this is really not about keys or buildings."

At this point every eye was on this senior saint whose entire life had been spent in ministry in the closing church. "This is about something a lot more important than buildings and keys." Ralph paused to open a package he had brought with him. From it he pulled out a framed plaque. "It's become popular in recent years for organizations and companies to craft a mission statement, and Bethel has also had its own mission statement. So today we're not really giving you keys to this building, as much as the mission of Bethel Evangelical Lutheran Church."

> "Today we're not really giving you keys to this building, as much as the mission."

He took the plaque, held it up, and read it aloud. The mission statement was a very straightforward, powerful expression of sharing the gospel, bringing transformation, and loving the community. It was the type of mission statement that any church which loves Jesus and wants to serve the gospel would be able to endorse. "Mark, we give our mission to New Life Community Church, to carry it forward into our community," he concluded.

There wasn't a dry eye in the place. The closing of the church was a reminder to everyone that this wasn't a death, nor was it really even a merger. It was a new means of carrying Christ's mission forward to reach a new generation.

Your Area as Well

As you consider your own situation, do you have relationships with other churches that are in need of a restart? Perhaps some of the stories in this chapter will lead you to begin exploring the possibilities of a partnership. Who knows, it may even lead to a new beginning for a church that still dreams of better years to come!

Mergers tend to be a unique form of church growth, typically happening one at a time. But there are other ways in which multi-site churches grow and expand, and sometimes we'll see the birth of two, three, or even four campuses at once. To witness this firsthand, let's trek westward to Vancouver, Washington (a suburb of Portland, Oregon), and explore what is happening in this highly unchurched section of the country.

12 TWO – OR MORE – AT ONCE

LIVING HOPE CHURCH

Vancouver, Washington

LIVING HOPE CHURCH

FAST FACTS

Church vision ▶	***Living Hope Church exists to passionately, authentically, and simply help people know and follow Jesus.***
Year founded ▶	***1996***
Original location ▶	***Vancouver, Washington***
Lead pastor ▶	***John Bishop***
Teaching model for off-sites ▶	***Primarily video/DVD***
Denomination ▶	***Nondenominational***
Year went multi-site ▶	***2006***
Number of campuses ▶	***17 US; 4 international***
Number of weekly services ▶	***24***
Worship attendance (all physical sites) ▶	***5,200***
Largest room's seating capacity ▶	***575***
Internet campus? ▶	***Yes***
International campus? ▶	***Yes***
Internet address ▶	***www.livinghopechurch.com***

Launching two or more campuses at once can help a church transition more quickly to a multi-site mind-set, as it engages the entire church in the process, creating even greater momentum. But the benefits should be weighed against the costs, since it can put a strain on both financial and human resources.

Ten years ago many churches were experimenting with multi-site options by adding satellite campuses and on-site venues. But for the most part, it was just that — an experiment, with little knowledge that others were exploring the same kinds of new models. As we indicated in our first book, *The Multi-Site Church Revolution*, multi-site church growth was initially more of a reactive strategy resulting from a lack of worship space or from city zoning challenges. Today, however, it has become a purposeful way of doing church, and the proactive strategies being deployed are aggressive moves for the advance of the gospel. Among these strategies is the acceleration model of launching multiple campuses at once.

We'll be spending some time with John Bishop and the team at Living Hope Church in Vancouver, Washington, to learn what happens when you intentionally launch multiple campuses at the same time. John and his team have done a multiple launch twice.

Dangerous. That's the word that comes to mind when I (Greg) think of John Bishop, lead pastor of Living Hope Church in Vancouver, Washington. I first learned of this church when my trusty Google Alerts surfaced a story on their proposed launch of five new campuses on one Sunday. When I emailed Geoff to ask him if he had heard of John Bishop, his quick response got right to the point: "Yeah ... and this guy is crazy!"

That reply turned out to be a bit of an understatement. Geoff's email included a link to a YouTube video of John Bishop experiencing a life-endangering moment with a Bengal tiger—and it had happened during a recent worship service! John had been using animal illustrations as object lessons in his family series called *Ark*, so he invited an animal trainer who runs a traveling zoo to bring a bunch of animals to church. John thought it would be a great way to draw families to the church, and he was right! It turned out to be a popular series. When the trainers brought out the full-grown tiger—complete with two handlers and a choker chain around his neck—John petted its neck as he would a cat. In response, the tiger stood up on his massive hind legs to lick John's face, resting his massive paws on John's shoulders, pulling John's head forward. There was John, face-to-face with a tiger's open jaw, and those outstretched paws pulling him closer. The handlers sprang into action, pulled them apart, and averted any possible danger (in case the tiger wanted to do more than just lick his new toy).

I like connecting with people who live on the edge, so I called John to set up a meeting. A few months later we met face-to-face, and I learned that John is indeed crazy and dangerous—crazy in love with Jesus and dangerous for the gospel.

John talked with me about his upcoming book, *Dangerous Church*, and his passion for reaching the lost. "Dangerous churches should be the norm," he said. "Church leaders and church people alike shrink back from danger because we want safety. Jesus said that he's overcome the world and its troubles. Dangerous churches put everything on the line for the one thing that matters most: *reaching lost people.*" Because the very mission Jesus gave his followers is "dangerous," John believes it's even more dangerous *not* to be a dangerous church that makes reaching lost people a top priority. Churches that seek safety end up missing out on the true excitement of working with God. "Living Hope is a church that is willing to risk everything to reach lost people," he said.

Birthed in 1996, Living Hope has exploded from five families to five thousand attenders, grown from one service to thirteen, gone multi-site, and baptized five thousand people along the way. The way John sees it, a dangerous church will experience the blessing of seeing what *"only God"* can do when they focus on doing what they are called to do — risk everything to reach people.

For Living Hope, launching five campuses at the same time was not a strategy for getting media attention. It was simply a way of being the church and responding to the call of Jesus to live a dangerous life for God. By the spring of 2006, Living Hope was experiencing rapid growth in worship attendance, but they found they were confined to a worship space that could seat only 575. Having maximized the number of services they could hold (there weren't any more time slots available), John pulled the church's lead team together and told them it was time to think outside the box. He led the way for his leaders by announcing an impossible vision — a five-campus multi-site launch on Easter 2006.

How Did It Happen?

With the vision cast, it was time to begin working. In just under three months, the Living Hope team developed a plan, built the teams, executed the logistics, and launched five campuses in and around the Vancouver area.

Missy Hannon, an executive pastor at Living Hope, provided leadership for the operational side of the launch. She recalls, "When John decided to launch five campuses, we got busy real quick. The model we were operating from was one that called for 'complete' campuses. We had to find facilities, staff, teams, and equipment to replicate the Living Hope experience."

They began by contracting with four movie theaters. Some were multiplex theaters, and the church moved forward, believing they had lined up the largest room at each location. "Then we found out just before Easter — four weeks out, after we had already launched the advertising — that the theaters weren't going to allow us to use the venues we wanted," Missy explains. "That was incredibly frustrating because at Easter, at every location, at every service, we had to turn people away."

After Easter, Living Hope scrambled and relocated, settling the five new starts into four brand-new locations, most of them rented school facilities. "We did a lot of changing in that first year," Missy says. "That happened in part because we were new to multi-site. But those were all good problems. If you outgrow something your first day, that's a great problem to have."

Part of the reason for the big crowds on Easter was the way John had intentionally made the launch a dangerous step of faith for the entire congregation. "It wasn't just five percent of the congregation that we asked to help," Missy explains. "Nearly one hundred percent of our people were involved. We sent core people to each of the new locations. It was something we all did together. Everyone drew energy from each other. We built a lot of momentum by partnering together, and everyone knew that they weren't in it alone."

The Next Big Risk

By the following year, with the new campuses just beginning to stabilize, John found himself wondering again, "What risk is God calling us to take this year if not to launch five more campuses? What vision is bigger than us? What is the *only God* initiative that we must undertake?" For John, taking a risk means pursuing something that will fail without God's involvement and believing that embraced risk leads to a revival of interest and passion. So John asked the question, "What are you asking of us this year, Lord?" And the answer came—Easter services at the Rose Garden, home of the Portland Trail Blazers. God was asking Living Hope to celebrate the resurrection in a twenty-thousand-seat NBA stadium.

With forty days and a fresh vision in place, the Living Hope leadership team kicked into gear, and Easter 2007 at Living Hope took place in the hallowed halls of the Blazers' home court. Over fifteen thousand people worshiped that Sunday, and around seven hundred individuals were baptized in what has now become a characteristic feature of worship at Living Hope—spontaneous baptisms. The Easter 2007 Rose Garden experience continued the mission of doing whatever it takes to bring lost people to Christ, while also showing the different campuses they could take a step of faith as one congregation to accomplish something none of them could do alone.

Risk Involves Release

One of the core beliefs at Living Hope is that embracing the risk of reaching out in faith-filled ways includes a commitment to release everyone for ministry. The "release everyone" principle was the hallmark of their Easter 2008 outreach. The risk involved an attempt to deploy all kinds of different people into all kinds of unique contexts throughout the community. One risky release involved a guy named Rick who had spent the majority of his adult life in a bar. In the very bar where Rick had sinned by embracing drunkenness and self-centered priorities, God gave him a platform to reach out with the love of Christ. A vision for *risking* led to a platform for *reaching* and eventually to *releasing* a man into full-time ministry. Rick, a relatively new but fully devoted follower of Jesus, is now a campus pastor for Living Hope Dodge City Saloon, a campus he started in a local bar. It's a campus that is now reaching people who wouldn't normally come to church but are willing to come to a place they know at the invitation of a person they know. Rick's visible transformation and his willingness to return are having a powerful effect on his community.

> A vision for *risking* led to a platform for *reaching* and eventually to *releasing* a man into full-time ministry.

Stories like Rick's are possible because John was willing to ask the question, "What dangerous risk of faith do you want this year, Lord?" Unwilling to sit back and simply enjoy the fruit of the previous year's Rose Garden experience, John had believed that the next big risk would involve another year of launching multiple campuses all on one day.

But it wouldn't be that simple. True to the mission of the church, there would be a new kind of danger in these launches. The church was reviewing their model of launching complete campuses, and John began to believe that their definitions were becoming a hindrance to the next risk God wanted them to take. As the church was growing and expanding in outreach, God was opening doors for new expressions of church that didn't fit into the standard, complete-campus launch. These were less-structured ways of engaging the community and could often occur more spontaneously than could the complete-campus model they were comfortable with.

The end result for Easter 2008, according to Missy, was a multiple-site launch that was both "outside of the box and much more organic and diverse." In addition to the campus launched in a bar were new sites in a homeless shelter chapel, a corporate office complex, the building of a struggling church, and an online campus on the internet. Over and above the variety of facilities used, the 2008 launches extended the ministry of Living Hope beyond the immediate region to include other states, such as Hawaii (I have humbly offered to serve as campus pastor there!), as well as countries such as New Zealand, India, the Philippines, and Mexico. The church is also in the midst of conversations about launching even more Living Hope campuses in India, the Philippines, and Mexico.

What did all these launches have in common? They were done not to simply grow numbers or have more buildings but as a means of releasing the people to be the church in the neighborhood and communities where they live. But the Easter 2008 initiative didn't stop there. Living Hope also broadcast services on a local television station so some Living Hope regulars could open their homes to do church in their neighborhood. While thousands of people unaffiliated with Living Hope viewed the services on television, approximately 150 Living Hope families hosted church in their homes, viewing the televised services and then discussing the content with unbelieving or unchurched friends and neighbors. At least one of these "house church" gatherings has now become the core for the launch of a future campus.

I asked Missy to compare the launches in 2006 and 2008. "The 2006 launches were highly structured," she said. "We told people, 'Here's your team of one hundred to serve as the core for your launch.' In contrast, 2008 was very organic. We said to people instead, 'Let's see what you can do with five people, with twenty-five, or with fifty.' In 2006 the greatest challenge was timing: how to manage the launch of five full campuses in five months from start to finish. In the 2008 launch, the management challenge was the loss of control. This was difficult for our team, but we came to believe that with the loss of control, we gained *exponential potential* for seeing more people come to Christ."

> "With the loss of control, we gained *exponential potential* for seeing more people come to Christ."

Permanent or Temporary?

You may have some questions at this point. After all, that's a lot of campuses launched over a very short three-year time period. You may be asking, "Is the 'dangerous church' model really sustainable?" I wondered that myself, so I asked John, "Do you see the campus launches over the last three years as permanent or temporary?" He answered that he believes most of them will be permanent. He admitted that there will be some attrition due to transitions in campus pastor leadership or in lost access to the hosting facilities, but the overall strategy at Living Hope is to launch locations that stick. "Don't forget, dangerous churches like Living Hope take risk, and risk by definition includes some failure," John reminded me. "But the risk is worth it as we strive to reach all people in every place with the inviting grace of Jesus Christ."

Why Should a Church Consider Multiple Launches?

Jim Tomberlin pioneered Willow Creek Community Church's regional multi-site model and currently serves churches as a multi-site advisor through his organization called Third Quarter Consulting. Jim believes that larger churches beginning the multi-site journey should almost always consider launching two or more campuses within six months of each other. "This gets the church to a multi-site mind-set faster and more fully engages the whole church, creating greater momentum," he says. Jim has worked with a number of churches on this model for launching multi-site. The Chapel at Grayslake, in the suburbs outside Chicago, launched four campuses in 2006, including one in the local jail, within six months of each other. Menlo Park Presbyterian in California launched its first satellite campus in a public high school in October 2007 and followed up with a second campus a few months later, in February 2008.

In addition to helping reinforce the multi-site mind-set, launching multiple campuses simultaneously increases the sense of ownership that church members feel toward the multi-campus model. In many ways, the experience of going multi-site is similar to the experience of having a new child. When the baby comes, everyone in the family pitches in to help with the new addition. Why? Because they *have to*; there aren't many options when you are trying to handle such a big change. In other words, it's a matter of necessity. The same could be said of churches that launch in multiple places. Because of the size of the task, there is a requirement for everyone to pitch in. And the old adage proves true — people have greater ownership in what they help build.

> The old adage proves true — people have greater ownership in what they help build.

Challenges

The most frequent challenge when launching multiple campuses simultaneously is financial. Missy Hannon at Living Hope says this was particularly the case in 2006 when they launched five complete campuses. "We launched all the campuses with a full complement of quality audiovisual, children's ministry equipment, and resources, not to mention full-time staff. That was expensive."

Jim Tomberlin indicates that in his experience, "though there is an obvious financial cost to launching multiple campuses simultaneously, the more significant cost is sending out significant volunteer leaders from the original campus. Churches that launch multiple campuses simultaneously are forced to raise up new leaders at the sending base, which is ultimately a good thing but can be scary in the early days of multiple church launches."

During the fall of 2006, The Chapel at Grayslake launched four campuses in a rapid four-month succession. Soon all the new campuses were flourishing. The attendance at the sending campus stayed about the same, but the loss of so many trained volunteer leaders left the original campus feeling very vulnerable. A year later the church had raised up new leadership at the original campus, and all the campuses were running effectively, although finances were very tight.

The personnel and managerial challenge involves both paid staff and volunteers. If a church's staff has a strong-performance track record and embraces a churchwide value of training others for ministry, it is usually able to handle the demands and rapid deployment of many volunteers. But if training leaders is not a core value of the church, be prepared! Likewise, if the church's leadership team has the ability to scale rapidly to a new level of complexity, there is a greater likelihood they will successfully navigate the challenge of simultaneous launches. But if everyone at the church is feeling maxed out, undertrained, and undersupported, you may run into some big problems if you try a multiple launch.

Counterpoint

Before you sign leases on five theaters for your next Easter multisite launch, let me (Geoff) share some of Seacoast's experience with multiple launches. On two occasions, we have launched two campuses within three weeks of each other. At Seacoast Church, we have decided *not* to embrace this model, having found that the challenges of multiple launches outweigh the benefits. Following are a few of the things we bumped up against.

1. The staff's attention is divided between multiple sites, and often each site feels that the other is getting the bulk of the attention.

2. The cost in leaders and resources is huge. This can be a tremendous drain on the sending campus and can take months and sometimes years to recover.

3. Newcomer follow-up is difficult because of the influx of new people and new leaders. It is very easy for people to fall through the cracks with so much happening at the same time.

4. After the launch weekend there are always a myriad of issues that arise. It is very difficult to troubleshoot challenges on several campuses simultaneously. Organization gets exponentially more complicated overnight. I would compare a multi-site launch to having twins or triplets. The logistics of going from no children to two or three all at once are very challenging. If you want to get a feel for what it's like to launch multiple sites simultaneously, try watching the popular TLC Network show *Jon and Kate Plus Eight*. It gives you a pretty good feel for what it's like to deal with multiple offspring at the same time.

5. Existing staff are usually stretched to the limit. The last time Seacoast launched two campuses simultaneously, our technical director, who oversaw the audio, video, and lighting systems at both campuses, almost collapsed from exhaustion.

Your Turn

So, is God giving you a dangerous vision for multi-site ministry? What risk is he calling you and your church to take for the gospel? Do you have a church culture focused on releasing people into ministry? Do you have the financial and human resources necessary to handle twins or triplets—simultaneous launches of multiple campuses? Or is your church better equipped to handle a single birth? This is a challenging decision in which prayer and following God's unique leading for your church is of the utmost importance.

As we've seen in this chapter, solid leadership is a constant factor in multi-site churches. And *capacity* is a key word for churches, especially when it comes to their leadership. In our experience, few people maximize the impact of leadership better than Steve Stroope. Our next journey takes us back to the South, where we'll meet with Steve, who serves as senior pastor at Lake Pointe Church in Rockwall, Texas.

13 MULTIPLIED, MULTIPLE LEADERS

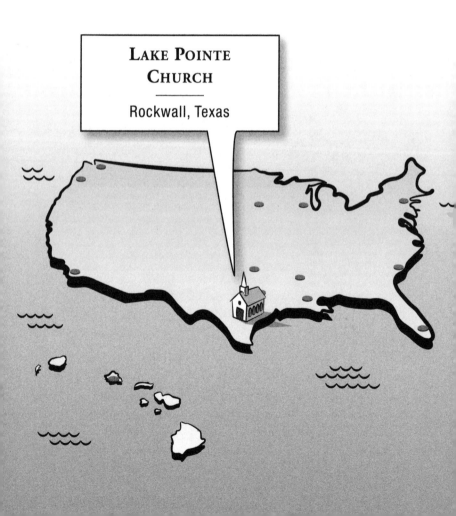

LAKE POINTE CHURCH

Rockwall, Texas

LAKE POINTE CHURCH

FAST FACTS

Church vision ▶	**To worship God and to share his great news with the surrounding community through authentic worship, teaching, and committed relationships.**
Year founded ▶	**1979**
Original location ▶	**Rockwall, Texas**
Lead pastor ▶	**Steve Stroope**
Teaching model for off-sites ▶	**Primarily video/DVD/satellite**
Denomination ▶	**Southern Baptist**
Year went multi-site ▶	**2004**
Number of campuses ▶	**7**
Number of weekly services ▶	**15**
Worship attendance (all physical sites) ▶	**11,433**
Largest room's seating capacity ▶	**4,700**
Internet campus? ▶	**No**
International campus? ▶	**No**
Internet address ▶	**www.lakepointe.org**

Good leadership is always the key to healthy, growing churches. That need multiplies and increases in multi-site churches. Effective multi-site churches have an established culture and well-developed strategies for reproducing and growing biblical leaders.

Leadership Network regularly surveys church leaders across North America. Consistently we are reminded of the importance of leadership development as a key factor in the effective ministry of the church. Not surprisingly, this finding is consistent with secular research as well. The strength of any organization, whether a church or a business, is greatly influenced by the strength of the leader. In a multi-site church, these leadership needs are intensified and expanded.

The other consistent discovery in Leadership Network's research is the urgent need for tools and processes to identify, equip, and release these leaders. As we spend some time with Steve Stroope of Lake Pointe Church, we'll get a chance to take a look under the hood of a well-oiled leadership development model and learn about some practical tools and processes for developing good leaders.

When I (Greg) recently visited Lake Pointe Church's original campus in Rockwall, Texas, it was a bit like going back home again. Rockwall is a community just east of where I live in Dallas, and my family and I had visited the church on numerous occasions throughout the years. But this time I entered the campus with a different set of eyes—my "leadership development scouting eyes."

On my visit, I couldn't help but notice all of the people volunteering that day as they greeted me, helped me find the appropriate classroom for our two boys, Daniel and Andrew, and led my wife, Susan, and me in worship and in an excellent time of teaching. It made me wonder about the history of this church when it came to recruiting and training volunteers. Are there more or less volunteers because the church is now multi-site? Are the volunteers better trained or more poorly trained since the multi-site transition? Is the church's intentionality about opening new campuses matched by an equal focus on making disciples through spiritual leadership development?

I've known Senior Pastor Steve Stroope for a long time. He's been a longtime friend of Leadership Network and an innovative leader for the church. At a lunch meeting later in the week, Steve updated me on Lake Pointe's growing multi-site presence as they have expanded to seven campuses:

1. The original campus in Rockwall continues to grow and houses most of the central operations that support the other locations.
2. The Town East campus, which was birthed out of a merger in 2004, is over 1,000 in weekend worship attendance. It meets in a renovated space formerly home to a large sporting goods retail outlet.
3. The Firewheel location, a 2007 merger, also has grown to over 1,000 worshipers each weekend.
4. They have a smaller campus in an outlying rural area.
5. Their most distinct venue is a "Cowboy Church," which reaches around 150 people each weekend.
6. Their venue at Dawson State Prison continues to serve 300 people each weekend, with many individuals coming to faith in Christ and then becoming a part of the Lake Pointe congregation upon completion of their terms.
7. The church's Buckner Terrace location is a collaborative effort that serves a neighborhood with an aging population and a changing ethnic demography.

Seven different locations translates into a need for lots of leaders, so I asked Steve if he had found a secret recipe for developing them. He affirmed that his staff are constantly addressing that very issue, and they ask themselves, "How can we identify, equip, and deploy leaders as rapidly as necessary to meet the demands associated with the huge opportunities that God is placing in our path?"

From the beginning of our work with multi-site churches, leadership development has been one of the most consistent themes among the questions we've heard churches ask. So what has Lake Pointe learned?

> From the beginning of our work with multi-site churches, leadership development has been one of the most consistent themes among the questions we've heard churches ask.

Always Looking for Leaders

One of the core practices in Lake Pointe's model is that they are *always* looking for leaders — twenty-four hours a day, seven days a week. Steve not only sees this as central to the success of a strong leadership development pipeline, but he also believes it is a foundational role of a biblical leader. He notes, "The Scriptures say that we are to equip the saints for ministry [Eph. 4:12]. The reason why most churches in America average less than 150 people is because that's about all one person can lead alone. The growth of the church is often stunted because they have ceased to live out the value of 'always looking for leaders.' In my twenty-eight years in ministry, there has never been a season when we did not need more leaders. The church is always in need of leadership and must always be looking for new ones."

> "There has never been a season when we did not need more leaders."

Lake Pointe labels this process as *discovery*, one of six components that together constitute their formal leadership development program. Discovery is the ongoing process of finding people who have the gift of leadership. It is fueled by this important principle: you are searching not just for today's leaders but also for those who will follow you. Steve believes that the best fishing pool for leaders is your current force of volunteers. In a sense, your current volunteers are really your farm team. In the major-league baseball systems, certain individuals with abilities and skills will surface from the minor-league farm teams. They are groomed and given more playing time to develop their abilities. In the case of the church, those who rise from the volunteer ranks are often given a greater span of ministry leadership. At Lake Pointe they may be called out to provide leadership at one of the church's campuses, serving in a variety of key roles.

A Culture of Leadership

Before we take a look at the other components in Lake Pointe's leadership development process, it is important to understand that this process doesn't operate in a vacuum. It's firmly embedded in and nourished by a healthy culture of leadership and leadership development. Steve is known around the church as a bit of a leadership nut, but his reputation is really just a reflection of his belief that "if you do not develop other leaders, the church suffers and it is limited in its capacity to touch its community and world, and potential leaders are robbed of the joy of doing what God designed them to do."

So the culture at Lake Pointe is shaped by Steve's passion and driven by his visionary modeling of leadership in every aspect of his ministry. This relentless pursuit of a consistent vision to raise up leaders has led everyone at Lake Pointe (staff and lay leadership alike) to understand that it's part of their responsibility to step up and develop other leaders.

The Rest of the Model

The remaining components of Lake Pointe's leadership development program include *connection*, *training*, *resourcing*, *coaching/mentoring*, and *celebration*. Each of these components are central to providing leadership for the broad range of ministries included in Lake Pointe's multi-site program, and each are replicated to scale on every campus.

The *connection* component is designed to help people find their sweet spot for serving. The importance of this piece of the puzzle is demonstrated by the presence of a church ministry center, located in the lobby on each of Lake Pointe's campuses. The ministry center provides tools that assist people in discovering their strengths and spiritual gifts. In addition, trained volunteers help people connect to an area of ministry that complements their gifts and wiring. One of the prominent features of this area is a "Top-Ten Volunteer Needs" board, and as you may have guessed, there are always plenty of multi-site ministry opportunities on the volunteer list.

The next component of leadership development *training* has two tracks. The first track involves specific tasks related to the job you are volunteering to lead. For example, if you were going to be involved on the tech team for the Firewheel campus, you would be trained to operate the sound board, the cameras, and other audiovisual resources used at that location. In addition to task-based training, there is the second track of the training component, which consists of general leadership training that the church provides through a series of courses offered by Lake Pointe University. These three-and-a-half-hour Saturday morning classes cover a broad curriculum that includes theology, discipleship, and other leadership issues like vision, values, and leading a team. In addition, web-based training is offered.

Closely tied to the training at Lake Pointe is the fourth component — *resourcing*. This involves sending leaders to both general and role-specific leadership conferences. The team also continually feeds their leadership base by giving or recommending the best books on leadership, using a designated shelf in the church bookstore. These books are available in the church library as well. The team believes that the use of common books helps provide corporate language and core concepts for everyone to use.

The *coaching/mentoring* component is the most relational one of the process. It is driven by the cultural rule that you cannot lead at Lake Pointe without an assistant. In every leadership role at the church, there is an assistant who regularly gets rotated into the front-line position they assist.

The final component—*celebration*—is often the most overlooked component of a healthy leadership development program, according to Steve. This is true because leaders are typically task oriented by nature, and they easily forget to make relationships a priority. Lake Pointe celebrates leaders by hosting quarterly huddles on their campuses, as well as an annual all-campus celebration in which testimonies are shared and individuals are affirmed and honored for their responsive leadership contributions.

Diminishing the Pool of Leaders?

Frequently, the multi-site model is critiqued by church leaders concerned that it will have the unintended consequence of reducing the number of qualified leaders in the church. After all, if you divide your leaders among multiple sites, how will you find new leaders? I raised this critique in my lunch meeting with Steve Stroope, who nodded—this wasn't the first time he'd heard that argument. Steve said, "I think it is actually exactly the opposite. Multi-site actually increases the pool of biblical leaders because in a multi-site model there are folks that have opened up to them a place to exercise leadership that would have been unavailable in one larger campus."

While we were writing this book, Ed Stetzer, popular author and president of LifeWay Research, posted a blog that expressed some of these very concerns. Do multi-site venues reduce the number of opportunities for people to serve? Doesn't video teaching tend to limit the number of ways in which leaders can develop communication skills? Good questions. In response to these concerns, Geoff highlighted four key points from his experience at Seacoast (which we've lightly edited):

1. While video venues may seem to reduce the opportunities available for people to preach and teach, there are still many multi-site churches that use in-person teaching. Even at churches that use video venues, there are often plenty of other opportunities for new leaders to develop their communication gifts.

2. At Seacoast, we have seen the exact opposite effect since we have opened multiple campuses; rather than a diminished pool of biblical leaders, we now have an ocean of biblical leaders. Every site we open creates multiple opportunities for emerging leaders to step up to the plate. I had lunch with a young man at one of our sites who has been on our youth staff for several years but now feels a desire to move into a larger role. In a traditional church he would have to leave and plant a church, because there would be few if any other opportunities for leadership within our church. Because we are a large, multi-site church, we were able to look at a wide range of leadership opportunities, from department leader to campus pastor to church planter. He is a biblical leader who is being groomed for big things down the road rather than put out on his own to sink or swim.

3. We have many biblical leaders who do not have the gift of teaching. It is surprising to me that biblical leadership and the ability to stand up and talk for thirty minutes on a Sunday somehow have become equated. It is also surprising that a thirty-minute homily is seen as the primary tool to speak into the lives of a congregation. At our campuses, the campus pastors lead and teach in dozens of ways every day; the only thing they don't do is teach for thirty minutes most Sundays.

4. We have also found multi-site to be a great way to prepare church planters. Naeem Fazal, who now pastors Mosaic Church in Charlotte, was our first campus pastor. It was a great leadership incubator, and Naeem now ministers to almost one thousand twentysomethings every weekend. He is one of many biblical leaders whom we have had the opportunity to develop through the multi-site ministry.[14]

Finding the Leaders of Fifty

Perhaps the most challenging shift for many multi-site churches comes when they have to live out the claims that they are empowering people for ministry. When you go to a multi-site model, you *really* have to dig deep. As David McDaniel of Atlanta's North Point Community Church said, "It's easy for someone to give up one kidney, but what happens when you want to give a second, third, and fourth?"

Robert Emmitt, the lead pastor from Community Bible Church (profiled in chapter 4), is a leader among leaders and a man of great passion. His vision is to have one hundred campuses over the next decade. And Robert is convinced that the driver and catalyst for that multi-site expansion will be leadership.

But Robert's insight is not simply an awareness of the need for more leaders; it's an understanding of where to *find* those leaders. "We moved to ten campuses rather quickly, and we did that by casting the net out and harvesting all the ready-to-go pastors we had," he said. "Now it's a matter of locating the next round of leaders, and we are convinced that we will find them both inside and outside our congregation. We will know they are a candidate if they are already leading a group of at least fifty and have a pastor's heart. We actually have lots of folks raise their hand to lead, but unless they are already leading a group of fifty as a volunteer, I'm not ready to lean on them to lead a campus."

Robert does not naively believe that these "leaders of fifty" are going to show up on the doorstep of Community Bible Church. Instead the next round of leaders must be found through a proactive search. One recent strategy involved hosting a weekend pastor's conference to whet people's appetites. The event cast the vision and described the opportunity for engagement in the multi-site ministry of Community Bible Church. In addition, Robert's multi-site director provides ongoing direction for a very intentional leadership recruiting and development track that prepares individuals for every aspect of serving in a multi-site campus. The six-week program instructs participants in the "why" of Community Bible's multi-site strategy as well as in the tactical and practical ministry skills needed to get started.

One additional source of leaders for Community Bible Church has been the relationships they have developed through a connection with Leadership Network's founder, Bob Buford. Many of these individuals, known as Halftimers—a term popularized by Bob's bestselling book by that same title—are approaching the midpoint stage of life, have had successful careers, and are now in a season in which they have capacity to be engaged in significant ministry. They often describe their experience as "moving from success to significance."

Community Bible's Brian Thomas is one such individual. Brian is the campus pastor of the Brook City campus in southeast San Antonio. He felt called to be a pastor twenty years ago but instead chose to pursue a secular career to support his family. Now serving as an executive with a large investment company, he also pastors a predominantly Hispanic campus.

Robert said, "I've got guys who are pastoring that never dreamed of being a pastor three years ago, but now they are. Terry Parks is pastoring Community Bible Church, Burney. He retired as CFO for a Fortune 500 company and came on staff with us. He's a wonderful leader who lived out in that area and felt called to start a campus. So now he's doing it and he loves it. And he's sixty-four years old."

Your Level of Leadership Development

How many people like Brian Thomas and Terry Parks are in your church, people with a heart for God *and* with leadership ability, who are capable of taking on larger leadership challenges? Is your church experiencing a growing need for multiple leaders to serve on multiple campuses?

> As *grows* the leadership, so *goes* the church.

If so, it might be time for a reality check about the leadership development program at your church. Do you have an intentional plan to develop leaders? As we've seen, it begins with the development of a leadership culture, often led by the senior pastor. Many of the systems and principles outlined in this chapter should assist you in developing a leadership pipeline that will work for your context. We're convinced that multi-site churches must remain focused on finding and developing biblical leaders. As *grows* the leadership, so *goes* the church.

The next stop on our multi-site roadtrip takes us up the Mississippi River to Minneapolis, Minnesota, home of Bethlehem Baptist Church. At Bethlehem we will explore the theological framework for a multi-site church. So pull out your Bible and put on your thinking cap as we head north to Minnesota, stopping momentarily in Louisville, Kentucky.

14 ARE YOU SURE THIS ISN'T A SIN?

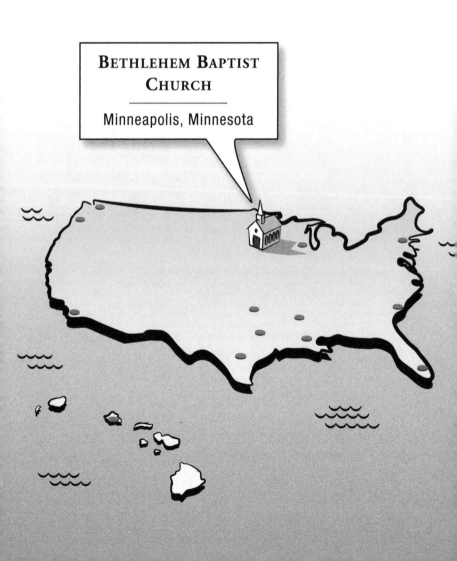

BETHLEHEM BAPTIST CHURCH

Minneapolis, Minnesota

BETHLEHEM BAPTIST CHURCH

FAST FACTS

Church vision ▶ **Spreading a passion for the supremacy of God in all things for the joy of all peoples through Jesus Christ.**

Year founded ▶ **1871**

Original location ▶ **Minneapolis, Minnesota**

Lead pastor ▶ **John Piper**

Teaching model for off-sites ▶ **Preacher rotates between campuses; other locations watch video/DVD from Saturday service**

Denomination ▶ **Converge Worldwide (formerly Baptist General Conference)**

Year went multi-site ▶ **2002**

Number of campuses ▶ **3**

Number of weekly services ▶ **8**

Worship attendance (all physical sites) ▶ **4,560**

Largest room's seating capacity ▶ **1,200**

Internet campus? ▶ **No**

International campus? ▶ **No**

Internet address ▶ **www.hopeinGod.org**

While some say going multi-site is simply a new opportunity to obey Jesus' great commission, others raise cautions. Are there biblical values that might be lost or weakened by the multi-site growth model?

I (Warren) remember a delightful visit I made to a two-campus church, Saint Stephen Baptist Church in Louisville, a predominantly African American congregation. I was greeted warmly and guided to a seat. After a time of vibrant worship and some well-produced video announcements, visitors were asked to stand, and then everyone was invited to hug one another. I received enough hugs to hold me for some while!

Later that morning I went to the church's other campus and followed the same drill: singing, announcements, and hugs, especially for newcomers like me. When I later asked the campus pastor why his church had gone multi-site, he referenced Acts 1:8 — where Jesus directs the church to be his witnesses in Jerusalem, Judea, Samaria, and ultimately the uttermost parts of the earth — noting that their second campus is their "Judea." He emphasized how much his church values the personal touch that leads to a personal decision of accepting Christ as Lord and Savior.

To me, the hugs were a symbol of their underlying theology: you can't win people unless you can touch them. "A flesh-and-blood appeal seems to be required," the campus pastor had agreed, explaining that's also the reason why they use in-person teaching — physically shuttling their senior pastor between campuses — rather than videocast.

John Piper: "Bible Neither Forbids nor Mandates"

For many churches, the biblical motivation for embracing the multi-site model isn't very controversial. Churches want to fulfill the Great Commission (Matt. 28:19–20) by giving more opportunities for the gospel to be shared. They want to obey the Great Commandment (Matt. 22:37–40) by taking the love of Christ to the people, meeting them where they are. These churches believe that new campuses are places where (to borrow the metaphors of Jesus in Luke 15) lost sheep and coins are sought out, and where lost children are welcomed home. They want to take big risks for God that don't violate Scripture, sharing the apostle Paul's dream that "by all possible means I might save some. I do all this for the sake of the gospel" (1 Cor. 9:22–23).

One church that has carefully and thoughtfully worked through the theological implications of going multi-site is Bethlehem Baptist Church. John Piper has served as the senior pastor of Bethlehem Baptist since 1980. For John, the issue of going multi-site was just one of many important theological discussions in the lengthy history of the church. Originally organized in 1871 as the First Swedish Baptist Church, the congregation held its first worship services exclusively in Swedish. Since those days, the church has dealt with the question of reaching out to non-Swedes, changing the language to English for worship, and relocating and expanding their facilities. Bethlehem is a church that takes its theology quite seriously, even to the point of selecting architectural design elements because of their biblical symbolism.

The church went multi-site in 2002, building a permanent north campus in 2005 and adding a southside campus in 2006. When John Piper spoke to the congregation about the church elders' decision to go multi-site, he emphasized two main points:

1. *Stewardship.* "Our first sanctuary, which lasted about 110 years, held 400. The current one holds 1,000. Is it better theology to build a bigger sanctuary, hope that an adequate amount of parking appears, and risk having an empty

albatross in coming years, or to develop multiple campuses, built for about 1,000 each, maybe 5 of them, covering perhaps 10,000 people total?"

2. *Evangelism.* "There are hundreds of thousands of people who are within driving distance of us and who, in not treasuring Christ, are not heading for heaven.... It's not an option for us to avoid thinking about those people."

"I don't think any text in the Bible forbids or mandates multiple campuses," John concluded. "Believing multiple campuses will yield more long-term effectiveness than the centralized enlargement of one downtown campus, we embraced the vision of a multi-campus church."[15]

Saint Stephen Baptist Church and Bethlehem Baptist Church represent many congregations with a high view of Scripture that have not found biblical objections to the overall idea of a multi-site church. Instead they believe that going to two or more campuses has helped them better live out the various mandates of a New Testament church.

Leaders from other traditions echo similar conclusions. For example, James MacDonald, pastor of Harvest Bible Chapel, a four-campus church based in Rolling Meadows, Illinois (which has also planted thirty-nine churches), says,

> Theologically I have no hesitation with multi-site. In fact, when I am up preaching, I will often say, "I'm glad that you are here today wherever you are worshipping. It doesn't matter where I am. All that matters is where you are and where God is, and He is right with you now as we open God's word together." The manifest presence of God in the corporate gathering of His people is significant, not the physical location of the mouthpiece, so to speak.
>
> There is definitely a multi-location dynamic to the church in Acts. And I don't see anything in Scripture that forbids it. And technology allows it and abundant fruitfulness tends to force it and church planting doesn't protect us from it. We arrived at it reluctantly because we can't discount it from Scripture.[16]

Friends Who Disagree

The multi-site movement does have critics, however. In this chapter, I want to listen thoughtfully to what certain skeptics have to say, especially the concerns raised by people who love God, care deeply about the church, want to reach lost people, and have a deep respect for Scripture as the Word of God. Just my kind of people!

Rather than setting up objections that can be knocked down with a sucker punch, let's look at the best arguments against the multi-site movement. The vast majority of these objections can be grouped into the following categories:

1. Preachers Don't Know People Personally

Some people feel that technologies like video teaching are replacing the personal relationship between preacher and local congregation. Everyone would agree that not all technology is good for the church, and so it is appropriate to ask about the theological implications and long-term effects of the way some multi-sites use video venues to replace in-person teaching.

In response, I wonder if the "pastor who knows me" notion has ever been reality for most churchgoers. As a child, I responded to an altar call by my pastor, but I did not have a personal relationship with him. As a teen, now in a new church, I rededicated my life to Christ at the conclusion of a message from my pastor, but I did not have a personal relationship with him either. Since I was a particularly rebellious teen, I made another public rededication of my life a couple years later, this time under the preaching of a guest pastor who did not know me. These shepherds may not have known their sheep by name, as perhaps only the Good Shepherd, Jesus, does (John 10:3, 11), but they certainly knew what wayward sheep are like, and they spoke in a language that this stray sheep could hear and understand!

I believe that these Bible teachers all could have taught via video if the technology had existed, just as people have come to faith by watching a Billy Graham telecast or listening to a recording from one of yesteryear's great gospel communicators. What matters, it seems, is not so much that the preacher knows me personally as that the teacher's message is biblically sound, applied in a way I can understand. Then hopefully the church has altar counselors, Sunday school teachers, youth group leaders, or other on-site people — as my churches did — to help disciple those who respond to the message. That's where the personal relationship is needed, through campus pastors and the teams they oversee!

2. Churches Are Just Following the Latest Fads and Trends

When people say, "Multi-site is just another fad," they are expressing a deeper concern that churches should avoid getting caught up in trying to be the latest and greatest thing to come along. Their concern is not so much an objection to the multi-site model as a wariness about naively hopping on a bandwagon or embracing something as right just because it's new.

We agree that doing what's right is always God's way, whether it's trendy or not. Some fads are bad, but others have theological merit. Bussing kids to Sunday school was a fad in the sixties and seventies, but it wasn't necessarily wrong. We don't support guilt by association — the logic that says that if it's a fad, it must be wrong. Instead we do support measuring each fad against the standards of God's Word.

3. Multi-Sites Make Church into a Show

Some people argue that multi-site churches are more event-oriented than single-site churches, with the result that they sacrifice true, biblical community. As one person emailed me, "The focus in multi-sites is often on the event more than the community, and people come for the show without connecting to the community."

I find this a difficult claim to sustain against multi-sites in particular. It does happen, regrettably, but in all kinds of churches. We have been unable to find any evidence that the typical multi-site with a campus pastor role places less emphasis on community than do regular, single-site churches. In our observations and conversations, we've learned that multi-sites must build community or they die.

4. There Are Going to Be Negative Outcomes

Some argue that multi-site churches lead to a loss of evangelism. But the facts clearly point otherwise. According to several Leadership Network surveys, multi-site churches are having a tremendous evangelistic impact.[17]

Some of the hardest objections to address are those based on the reality that we simply don't know what the long-term effects of the multi-site movement will be. The core argument is often, "Doing multi-site will [or might] lead to

> In our observations and conversations, we've learned that multi-sites must build community or they die.

…" This is where honest disagreements occur, since only God knows with certainty where some things in this movement will lead. Examples include:

▶ The multi-site approach will hurt existing smaller churches in a community.

▶ Multi-sites cater too much to American consumerism and might create an even more consumeristic attitude.

▶ Multi-sites elevate one leader too prominently, and if that leader falls, the ripple effect will be multiplied across all the campuses.

▶ Multi-sites appeal to people in a society that likes name-brand recognition, but when the culture shifts to preferring boutique-style stores, multi-sites will begin to flounder.

One of the most thoughtful, stimulating, and lively discussions of these "what-if" concerns about multi-site can be found in the online discussion thread on Ed Stetzer's post from June 2008.[18] Geoff was one of the primary respondents (as chapter 13 mentioned). While

I appreciated what both Ed and Geoff said in the post, I was most impressed by this comment from a pastor responding to the argument that the multi-site models might lead to a bad outcome: "The bottom line is that if the sending church is lacking in any of these areas, the satellites will be lacking also. But if the sending church is strong, outward-focused, and developing healthy networks of care and community, then the satellites will do well in these areas. After all, we're not out to replicate a church service, we're out to replicate the entire life of the church. That includes healthy vertical and horizontal relationships."

The key idea is simple and biblical: bad trees bear bad fruit, but good trees bear good fruit, as Jesus said in Matthew 7:15–20. There are actually some churches that we have tried to discourage from going multi-site. When the church is not healthy, it's not a wise idea to spread that illness by starting a new campus. It's like trying to fix a bad marriage by having a baby. Cure the sickness in the church before you consider reproducing.

5. Multi-Sites Fail to Make Disciples

Some say that multi-site churches shift the focus to producing spectators rather than disciples and leaders. In other words, the multi-site paradigm, without intentionally working otherwise, will limit reproduction of leadership at every level.

We wholeheartedly agree that any model fails if it doesn't make disciples as Jesus commanded in Matthew 28:18–20. Any church is at fault, whether single-site or multiple-site, if it allows the leader to do the ministry while everyone else watches.

Again, our experience with multi-site is that disciple making does occur. In fact, multi-site churches do not survive long unless they put feet to their words about developing the people of God into leaders who reproduce themselves through others, as Paul illustrates in 2 Timothy 2:2's statement about the need to train others, who in turn train others, who in turn train others. If multi-site churches don't empower God's people for ministry, they fail. Some of the most exciting multi-site churches model an explosion of new opportunities for God's people to do hands-on ministry, opportunities that provide a great context for discipleship.

For instance, consider Molly Cunningham. Molly was a key volunteer and leader at Crossroads Community Church in Cincinnati, Ohio, beginning with their core group in 1996. Her first staff role was with the church's first youth group and over time she led a number of different ministries at the church, including outreach ministries, community groups, first impressions, and adult spiritual formation.

> If multi-site churches don't empower God's people for ministry, they fail.

For a number of reasons, it seemed like a great fit for Molly to become a campus pastor when the church opened its second campus. "Crossroads is all about mobilizing people," Molly says, "and that fits what I'm about. I love to get leaders on board with the vision God is calling our community to."

Crossroads' primary approach to assimilating newcomers is to get people engaged in serving, something they can begin anytime, with no prerequisites. The logic is to mix seekers with revolutionary Christ followers. The church's in-house term for that approach is the fusion model.

"My role is a developer/talent scout for volunteer leaders," Molly says. Week after week she does just that at one of the Crossroads campuses.

To us, the development of volunteers like Molly gives practical evidence that good things can come from a multi-site approach. For those who are evaluating the potential merits of multi-site, the opportunity to provide God's people expanded opportunities to live out the Great Command and the Great Commission tips the scale in favor of the multi-site approach.

What about Your Church?

If you are moving forward into the multi-site model, are you clear on the biblical values you believe it is advancing? Are you aware of the liabilities to guard against? How strongly have your leaders and congregation connected the dots between the core principles of God's Word and the potential outcomes of becoming one church in more than one location? Don't overlook the essential foundation of helping people understand why you do church the way you do.

One of the most persuasive fruits from multi-site churches is the presence of spiritual grandchildren. That reproductive multiplication is what moves something from a model to a movement. To find out what we mean, fill up the gas tank one more time, and let's go back to Seacoast.

SEACOAST CHURCH

Mount Pleasant,
South Carolina

Many churches are moving from addition to multiplication as secondary campuses begin launching campuses of their own. This new wave of "grandchildren" increases the challenges of DNA transfer.

On our multi-site roadtrip, we have visited fourteen churches in thirteen different states. We've mentioned several others in passing. Taken all together, that's just a fraction of the churches we could have visited. Multi-site churches now exist in at least forty-seven states and in Canada's four largest provinces.

As we enter the final stretch, let's wrap up back where we started, in Charleston, South Carolina. While you're in town, make sure you try the shrimp and grits (it's better than it sounds) as we take a look at what happens when campuses birth their own campuses.

I (Geoff) am part of a unique family—we all are! Some of our families have an inordinate amount of circus clowns, some are full of Chicago Cubs fans, and in some families, they don't drink Diet Coke. Yes, every family has its own hardships and burdens to bear. One of the unique things about my family is that we have an abundance of pastors. We are literally infested with full-time ministry professionals. There are Surratts who pastor on the West Coast, the East Coast, and several coasts in between. Some of us pastor big churches, some little churches; some are senior pastors, some assisting pastors.

But the one thing that draws all of us together is our connection to E. L. Surratt. He was my grandfather.

E. L. was not the kind of guy you'd pick to produce a herd of pastors. He grew up far from the church and even farther from God.

He was a sharecropper, a bootlegger, and an all-around mean person. Then one day God knocked him down, literally, in the middle of the street. He had just walked out on his wife, who had recently committed her life to Christ in a Pentecostal tent revival, and had let her know in no uncertain terms that he wasn't going to spend the rest of his life with a "holy roller." Half drunk, flat on his back in the middle of a red dirt road in western Oklahoma, E. L. called out to a God he barely believed in and asked for a second chance at life.

E. L. joined the local church and threw himself into learning everything he could about God. Most of his subsequent education came from listening to sermons; he had only a sixth-grade education, so reading was never a strong point.

When the dust storms swept across Oklahoma, E. L. was forced to uproot his family and move to California to find work. He picked fruit, mended fences, built buildings — anything to put food on the table for his wife and three young children.

Eventually he saved up enough money doing contract work for the government during World War II to buy a small grocery store and gas station in Visalia, California. Once again he threw himself into church, and soon he became an unpaid assisting pastor at the local Assembly of God church.

Soon he felt a tug on his heart to return to Oklahoma and plant a new church. He wrestled for a long time with this idea. How could an uneducated, former heathen pastor a church? Over time the feeling became so strong that he sold everything he owned, uprooted the family again, and moved halfway across the country back to Oklahoma.

My grandfather spent the rest of his life planting and pastoring small churches across Oklahoma and beyond. If you were to focus on just the things he was able to accomplish in his lifetime, you would probably conclude that his impact on the kingdom of God was minimal. He never led an influential congregation, never wrote a book, and he never spoke to a crowd of more than five hundred people in his life.

But you'd be wrong about his impact. Even to this day it continues to grow. Twenty years after his death, the movement he started is exploding.

How? Because he had grandchildren.

Each of E. L.'s children became pastors or married pastors. They led moderate-size churches across the Midwest and southwestern United States. Ten of E. L.'s grandchildren also became pastors and today lead congregations across the country. Even seven of his great-grandchildren are now working in full-time ministry. Thousands of people across the United States are now being influenced by E. L.'s family every weekend. What started on a dirt road in a tiny town in Oklahoma is now reaching people from coast to coast and around the world.

Movements are always sustained by the third generation. Visionary leaders can easily inspire a group of people to follow them. Sometimes those followers will take up the message and inspire others, but sometimes they don't. And if they don't, that new, revolutionary idea will die. It takes "grandchildren" for a movement to gain legs. My grandfather's legacy is now assured because it has been passed on to the third and fourth generation. His grandchildren and great-grandchildren will continue to tell his story again and again (as I do, telling another portion of his story in *The Multi-Site Church Revolution*, page 67). Thus his values are passed on from generation to generation.

> Movements are always sustained by the third generation.

The same is just as true in a multi-site church. The lasting power of a multi-site church is seen, not when they plant campuses, but when those sites also begin to reproduce. When the original site is no longer the only source for new campuses, but you have campuses reproducing campuses, you have arrived at the third generation—multi-site grandchildren!

Seacoast Grandchildren

We are beginning to see this happen at Seacoast. Our church has experienced the birth of three grandchildren so far in our multi-site journey. The first was born just a few months after we opened our first off-site location, called the Annex. The Annex was geared toward college students and young adults, and it quickly filled to capacity after opening on Easter of 2002. The rapid growth of that campus prompted some Annex leaders to begin thinking ahead: what would happen if they opened a site on or near the campus of the College of Charleston? They did some research, found a hall that the college was willing to rent for a reasonable rate, and in January 2003 we welcomed our first grandchild.

> The lasting power of a multi-site church is seen, not when they plant campuses, but when those sites also begin to reproduce.

The grandchild's vibe was completely different from any of our other sites. The band was more edgy and ragged. The worship leader tended to show up late, as did a good part of the setup team. The crowd, made up entirely of college students, always seemed a little tired when the service began (from late nights of studying, I'm sure), and the dress code was, as you might expect, extremely casual.

Seacoast's second experience with grandchildren happened one hundred miles up the road in Columbia, South Carolina. After opening the Columbia campus in fall 2002, the campus pastor at that location had a vision to expand into another part of town. He found another leader and helped him gather a planting team from within the Columbia congregation. In fall 2003 Seacoast Irmo was born. Today it is even larger than its parent campus.

Seacoast's third grandchild was born on Easter 2007 at James Island, South Carolina. Seacoast's central support team helped with the logistics of launching the new campus, but the hands-on recruiting and training of the core team and the campus pastor happened at the West Ashley campus, which had been launched in 2003.

Danger of Grandchildren

In the movie *Multiplicity*, Michael Keaton's character creates a clone of himself. It's the perfect solution: his clone can go to work and do the boring chores of life, and he can hang out and have fun. Eventually Keaton discovers that his clone has created his own clone, who turns out to be quite goofy. When Keaton asks for an explanation, clone number one states the obvious: "You know what happens when you have a copy of a copy."

Sadly, that's a very real problem when you have campuses reproducing campuses: the original DNA can sometimes become altered. The second-generation campus may clap their hands during worship a little more than the original campus does. The third-generation campus may clap their hands *and* jump up and down. And a fourth-generation campus may decide to swing from the chandeliers (which can be very disturbing to the original worship committee).

> Birthing a third-generation campus forces the second-generation campus to rethink how they do things, opens them up to new ideas, and revitalizes the core.

Another challenge with grandchildren is the distance of their connection to the original campus or to central support. When our James Island campus pastor has a question, his first instinct is to ask someone at the West Ashley campus rather than someone at central support, and the answer he gets may or may not match what central support would say. When West Ashley says "always" and central support says "never," it leads to an intense level of fellowship as we sort things out.

All this is not to discourage you from having your campuses reproduce. It's just a heads-up that a church should decide how much control they want over the third-generation campuses before considering the grandchild route. Neil Cole, author of *The Organic Church*, recently reminded me that as long as the entire DNA is contained in the seed of the new church or campus, there is no need to worry about what will grow. If you are willing to allow for some minor anomalies, campuses reproducing campuses can have some big upside potential.

Grandchildren Can Rock Your World

As with my grandfather, the biggest advantage of grandchildren campuses comes from the multiplication factor they represent. When Seacoast's original campus began launching campuses, we were able to add new believers, new artists, and new volunteers. When all thirteen campuses begin to reproduce, we see multiplication at work on a very exciting scale. Instead of hundreds of new believers, artists, and volunteers, we can talk about thousands. When we move from addition to multiplication, the potential impact is incredible.

Leadership development is also ramped up when campuses begin to reproduce. At Seacoast, all campus pastors know that part of their job is to identify and train the next generation of campus pastors. We seldom hire from the outside, so campus pastors are focused on finding the right people from within their own congregation. Leadership is also diffused throughout the organization. Campuses that have reproduced are responsible for not only their own campus but also the campus they have launched. This type of responsibility helps leaders see the big picture and mature in their leadership.

Grandchildren also tend to keep you young. They are a constant source of new ideas. They tend to think in different ways than their grandparents do. They aren't always aware that something can't be done, so they don't care that it has always been another way, and they aren't all that worried about failing. With children like that, the launching campus gains almost as much benefit as the campus being launched. Birthing a third-generation campus forces the second-generation campus to rethink how they do things, opens them up to new ideas, and revitalizes the core.

How to Get Grandchildren

1. *Loosen your grip.* Is your church open to less control and more diversity? Encouraging campuses to launch additional campuses will stretch your identity and open up a lot of variation from your original blueprint. Are you comfortable with that?

2. *Build it into your DNA.* Begin to talk about reproduction from the very first day you launch a new campus. Encourage the local leaders to begin identifying their potential successors from the start. Document what needs to be reproduced, so future generations have a plan to work from without direct supervision.

3. *Find a way to fund it.* Someone once said that planning without funding is just daydreaming. How can you create a monetary source that is available for campus launches? Perhaps it could be a part of your next capital campaign, or you might challenge some of your bigger givers to dedicate some funds to a campus start-up fund. When it comes to having grandchildren, if you pay for it, they will build it.

4. *Affirm what happens.* Encouragement and permission granting go a long way. If you've been praying for your offspring campus(es), follow the lead of the Holy Spirit in how you counsel them and train them in the Bible's teachings. Then you can trust God in how your grandchild looks, and even for the timing of the birth.

Not Just Seacoast

Seacoast is not the only multi-site church to have had grandchildren. The New Hope Leeward campus profiled in chapter 2 has also opened other campuses, making New Hope Honolulu a grandparent. LifeChurch.tv, profiled throughout this book, has seen two more campuses launch from their Tulsa campus.

While we may not be the only multi-site grandparent, we didn't just wait around before trying to encourage the birth of grandchildren. In an actual family, it's usually a good idea to wait until your kids grow up, get married, and gestate for nine months before you begin celebrating the birth. But with churches, the process can move much faster. It's all about vision, opportunity, and faith-backed action.

The First Generation

This decade has seen the birth of more multi-site congregations than has any era in U.S. history, so most are only in the first and second generations—parents and children, but no grandchildren. Our best estimate of the number of multi-sites in this country, based on various interviews and facts collected through Leadership Network, is seen in the historical breakdown:

Number of Known Multi-Site Churches in the United States (one church in two or more locations)	
1700s	fewer than 10
1800s	fewer than 20
1900–1970s	fewer than 50 (mostly off-site preaching points and Sunday schools that developed accompanying worship services)
1980s	fewer than 100 (same)
1990s	about 200 (in addition to the above, a small number of churches began experimenting with having multiple campuses)
2000	300
2001	400
2002	600
2003	800
2004	1,000
2005	1,200
2006	1,500
2007	2,000
2008	2,500
2009	3,000

As we predicted in *The Multi-Site Church Revolution*, and as we still believe, the day will soon arrive (and may already be here) when multi-site is seen as the new normal. Today it's fairly normal for churches to offer multiple service times; no one raises an eyebrow when a church goes from one service to two or more. We believe that the day is coming when multi-site becomes the normal way many churches grow and expand to reach out to their communities.

This progression will only happen, however, if the practice of birthing grandchildren campuses becomes widespread. We are confident that it's just a matter of time before the kids start having kids, but time is no guarantee of success. We must not forget that it's essential for churches to embrace a vision for replication and multiplication, fueled by the confidence that more people will come to know Christ as we bring the church to them in a way they understand.

PREDICTIONS OF WHAT'S NEXT

The multi-site movement has developed and accelerated at a dramatic pace over the last twenty years, but we suspect we've only begun to identify some of the far-reaching implications of this movement. So what's on the horizon? Here is our list of predictions. We've tried to incorporate opinions from several church observers, especially our good friend Jim Tomberlin (introduced on page 150).

1. *Campus pastors are becoming a new widely accepted role.* The campus pastor role is becoming a strategic and sought-after church staff position. People may ask initially, "If they don't preach, what *do* they do?" Then after a learning curve, church members and staff alike are drawn to the strengths of this new role. It's turning the definition of a pastor upside down for many congregations. Rather than looking for seminary-trained professional speakers, churches look internally for leaders with a heart for ministry and corresponding leadership gifts.

2. *Church planters will play a significant role in creating new variations of multi-site effectiveness.* Multi-site was initially perceived as a celebrity pastor vehicle for building an empire. Now it is increasingly seen as a viable way of starting new churches. Established churches are also catching the reproducing/multiplying church bug, using multi-site as a preferred method—new campuses that become new churches.

3. *Variety in multi-site locations will continue to proliferate.* Many churches took their first step into multi-site in the most obvious locations—the new fast-growing suburb where many of

the church's families already live, the university across town where the church already has good inroads, etc. For a rising generation of pastors, it's not about whether or not they should go multi-site; it's a question of when and how. Pastors and churches will continue to experiment with this model. Distant campuses in multiple states or even rural areas will also become more common.

4. *International campuses will help transform approaches to missions.* The model of two-way partnering between North American and overseas churches will become more direct, relational, and personal as churches define what it means to have a campus overseas. Missionaries will be assisted as more people from their sponsoring churches become engaged in cross-cultural missions.

5. *Churches will grow bigger but will meet in smaller venues.* Megachurches will continue to grow in number and size, but the majority of their attenders will meet in multiple smaller facilities. Rather than constructing one huge auditorium, these churches will build or rent smaller buildings of five hundred to fifteen hundred seats. These churches may also add multiple venues at many of those locations.

6. *New believers will view their church location like branch banking.* Generations ago people chose in their town between First Baptist, Second Baptist, and Third Baptist (or Presbyterian, Methodist, etc.). Now they're more likely to choose between Community Church's west campus, north campus, and south campus. New believers will increasingly identify with a church brand, picking one campus as their base but being comfortable with an occasional stop at another "branch" location.

7. *Connections by video, from webcams to high-definition cameras, will become commonplace.* A society used to jumbotrons at sporting events and image magnification at other large-crowd events is already very accepting of video-projected teaching, with HD becoming standard for video presentation of

worship. You may not believe it, but holographic 3-D preaching is coming sooner than you think, and you won't even need those special glasses to experience it! Two-way video between church sites will also become relatively easy. Small groups will commonly use an internet connection for teaching, making geographical differences between the teaching site and the group almost irrelevant.

8. *Some multi-site churches will go double-digit in their number of campuses, and a few will go triple-digit.* Most multi-sites will continue to sponsor only two or three campuses, but a number will find that a multi-site approach perfectly matches their calling and mission, and they'll master the scale necessary to develop ten, twenty, fifty, and even a hundred or more campuses. They will learn how to do so for a fraction of the cost of constructing larger buildings, an idea that will have particular appeal each time their region faces an energy crisis or economic pinch.

9. *Multi-site models will help smooth out two typically rough transition points: declining churches and longtime pastors facing retirement.* Church mergers, acquisitions, and adoptions are increasingly becoming a staple in the multi-site movement and will transform the church landscape across North America. This will happen everywhere from city churches to rural churches. Likewise, senior pastor succession in long-term or high-visibility situations will find much appeal in the team-teaching approach that multi-site can offer.

10. *Internet campuses will be accepted as legitimate.* Churches will continue to find ways to increase interactivity, just as general social networking sites are doing. The idea of relationship-rich community, where caring, serving, and outreach occurs, will blur between in-person and online events. Churches of all sizes will move from posting their teaching online toward developing full-fledged internet campuses.

11. *Multi-site will gradually become more mainstream with denominations.* Although the initial wave of multi-site churches

were disproportionately nondenominational, more and more denominational churches will explore multi-site as a strategy for church revitalization.

12. *A few multi-site churches will become mini-denominations.* This is most likely to happen with those that use centralized teaching or self-written children's curriculum and that expand beyond their region. Many of these will add international campuses. The challenge of tracking churches that have multiple locations, some of which plant daughter churches, will cause great confusion for all kinds of statisticians. New terms will emerge to minimize double counting of attendance, baptisms, or budgets. Plus, accountability systems that are geographically based will evolve to accommodate churches that are no longer limited to one area. An entire new family of consultants and church service industries will emerge to serve multi-site networks.

13. *Authors who write books in the style of a roadtrip tour will …* Well, you tell us what you think the future will be! Please offer your thoughts on the ideas of this book, especially this chapter, and continue the conversation with us at our official blog, which continues the work of our companion book, *The Multi-Site Church Revolution.* The blog is www.multisiteroadtrip.com.

ACKNOWLEDGMENTS

We're thankful to more than one hundred different multi-site churches that one, two, or all three of us have visited in recent years. We're grateful for your time, hospitality, and willingness to share what God has been teaching you. Many of those churches are listed in the index of churches.

We're thankful to our families for allowing us to visit so many churches — individually, on family vacations, and through business trips, especially through Leadership Network.

We cannot speak highly enough of the opportunities Leadership Network (www.leadnet.org) has provided us to have close access to so many innovative multi-site churches. We especially thank founder Bob Buford, president Tom Wilson, managing director Dave Travis, conference planner Todd Rhoades, digital guru and Leadership Community director DJ Chuang, multi-site church tracker and amazingly thorough fact-checker Julia Burk, uber-organizer and project manager Stephanie Plagens, church information finder Bonnie Randle, and database manager Cynthia Beal.

The Zondervan team has been a joy to work with, including Paul Engle, Ryan Pazdur, John Topliff, Chris Fann, Brian Phipps, and others.

Finally, we enjoyed making many friends through the blog www.multisiteroadtrip.com, and we look forward to making more friends there in the future. See you on our next roadtrip!

RESOURCES

There are lots of places you can go to learn more about the multi-site approach to church:

▶ Our previous book, *The Multi-Site Church Revolution*, does not duplicate what you've read in this book. Instead we wrote the two as companions to each other. *The Multi-Site Church Revolution* is more of an overview and how-to manual, while this book is more of a series of drill-downs on particular multi-site themes.

▶ Leadership Network offers several dozen free downloads—concept papers, research reports, and podcasts—at www.leadnet.org/multisiteresources.

▶ Our blog, www.multisiteroadtrip.com (same as www.multi sitechurchrevolution.com), includes several hundred postings, including dozens of free resources.

▶ Free downloads of the Multi-Site Exposed conference are available at www.multisiteexposed.com.

▶ See www.multi-site.org for the Coast-to-Coast series of multi-site conferences.

▶ Subscribe to Jim Tomberlin's free newsletter *Multi-Sightings* at www.ThirdQuarterConsulting.com.

We're often asked for ministry descriptions that will work for multi-site churches, especially regarding the role of campus pastor.

Our blog offers you some additional campus pastor job descriptions and can be accessed at www.multisiteroadtrip.com. Here are three examples to get you started:

1. Granger Community Church (www.gccwired.com)

Summary

The Campus Pastor is the "face" of Granger Community Church (GCC) at a regional campus. He or she is a high-capacity leader who builds teams to ensure the success of the local campus. Success is defined as a growing campus fulfilling the vision of GCC by helping people take their next step toward Christ — together.

Role: The Campus Pastor is a ...

- ▶ Catalytic Leader: Able to rally people to a cause.
- ▶ Team Builder: Can build teams and identify high-capacity leaders to build more teams.
- ▶ Relational Leader: Friendly and approachable.
- ▶ Talent Scout: Always on the lookout for new leaders and volunteers.
- ▶ Total Quality Manager: Looking for ways to improve; sensitive to misses; committed to excellence.

▶ Communicator: The primary host, greeter, and vision-caster of this congregation.

▶ Cheerleader: Encouraging volunteers and staff constantly.

▶ Carrier of the DNA: When you cut them, they bleed the mission, vision, and values of GCC.

▶ Solution Specialist: Able to identify problems and find solutions.

▶ Staff Champion: Cares for the spiritual, emotional, and familial health of campus staff.

▶ Pastor: Has a heart to identify leaders and build systems to care for the congregation.

▶ Reproducer: With the entire staff, reproduces leaders, followers of Christ, and campuses.

Personally: The Campus Pastor is a ...

▶ Learner: Can take direction and feedback well and has a great desire to learn.

▶ Seasoned GCCer: Knows GCC, loves GCC, no question on understanding method or philosophy.

▶ Conflict Resolver: Unafraid to tackle interpersonal conflicts, ministry misalignment, or issues of sin.

▶ Leader at Home: No concerning spiritual or emotional health issues within his or her family.

▶ Time Manager: Does not require external systems to prioritize; is intrinsically motivated.

▶ Person of Integrity: At the core, they make solid decisions based on lifelong values.

▶ Self-Aware Individual: Knows where he or she is weak—finds others to fill in those gaps.

▶ Disciple: Fully devoted to following Jesus in everything they do.

Job: The Campus Pastor ...

▶ Pastors: Helps meet the care needs of his/her growing congregation. Some of this is done personally. As the church grows, much of this is done by developing systems of care and equipping leaders to help.

▶ Is Present: Keeps a presence in the community where the campus is located. Lives near enough to be able to easily be available to hold meetings or respond to needs in the community.

▶ Builds Teams: Identify, equip, empower, and lead volunteers to do the ministry of the church at this campus.

▶ Connects: Attends the all-staff meeting at the Granger campus each week; Meets with members of the senior management team individually or as a group as requested.

▶ Communicates: Keeps his/her supervisor aware of the successes and struggles taking place at the site by proactively and consistently sharing stories and reports.

▶ Is an Expert: He or she learns the people, issues, needs, concerns, history and demographics of the community.

▶ Is Flexible: Jumps in to help wherever needed at any of GCC's campuses or ministries.

▶ Adheres: To the GCC staff handbook which includes our statement of ethics.

▶ Follows: A leader, yes, but also a follower who will do everything possible to make their supervisor, the senior pastor, and the leadership at GCC a success.

Success of a Campus: Defined by ...

▶ Making Disciples: People are meeting Jesus and growing in their faith.

▶ Passionate Alignment: There is excitement about the vision of GCC.

▶ Growing Intentionally: Every year, more people are attending, meeting Christ, taking steps and participating than were in the previous year.

▶ Financial Health: Within twelve months, the revenue coming in matches or exceeds the expenses going out. Within twenty-four months, the excess revenue coming in has paid for the start-up expenses.

▶ Volunteer Development: The ministry is led by capable, trained, and aligned volunteers.

▶ Collaborative Creativity: The campus becomes a "petri dish" for creativity and innovation, and the ministry that flourishes is shared with all the other campuses.

▶ This campus is led by the campus pastor, but he or she is not alone in achieving success at that campus. The senior management team and the entire staff of GCC will be working for the success of each campus.

Accountability

▶ Reports: To the Director of Multi-Site

▶ Responsible For: Any staff hired at the same campus; All volunteer leaders at that campus.

▶ Category: Full-time, Associate Staff

2. Liquid Church (www.liquidchurch.com)

Summary

Do you have the kind of leadership that has people following you anywhere? Are you a rock star networker? Does the thought of inspiring those around you to do more than they ever thought they could, fill you with excitement? Do you relish the thought of joining a talented team of next generation leaders that's making a massive difference for Christ?

You Are

▶ A proven leader with a knack for public speaking

▶ A strong communicator and motivated team-builder

▶ Passionate about recruiting and leading volunteers

▶ Experienced in leadership roles in either a church or corporate environment

▶ A multi-tasker, but can follow through and get things done

▶ Organized and able to stay on top of administrative duties

- Hard-working, but know how to laugh and have a good time
- Self-confident, secure and more passionate than power-hungry
- A team player no matter what
- Committed to the ministry philosophy and core values of Liquid Church

You Will Be

- Responsible for assisting in the administrative supervision of a campus
- An instrumental part of developing Life Group leaders and coaches
- An instrumental part of building teams, developing leaders and volunteers
- Performing pastoral care responsibilities such as weddings, funerals, baptisms, and child dedications

If you're convinced you're the right person for the job, send us your resume and convince us. Bonus points if you include a DVD, video, or website link demonstrating your skills.

3. Sagebrush Community Church (www.sagebrushcommunity.com)

Primary Responsibilities

- Leader: Provides direct oversight of all operations and staff of the Sagebrush campus.
- Emcee: Serves as the "face with the place" and emcees before and after each service.
- Shepherd: Provides standard pastoral duties to those attending/related to the campus.
- Centurion: Oversees small groups and their leaders affiliated with this particular campus.
- Mentor: Provides leadership to paid and volunteer staff and oversees all ministry teams.

▶ Organizer: Ensures quality control, excellence, and efficiency of all campus operations.

▶ Recruiter: Serves as a talent scout for new leaders and volunteers and connects them.

Minimum Requirements

▶ Ministry experience (even as a volunteer) for at least three years.

▶ Member of Sagebrush Community Church for at least one year.

▶ Full support of the Sagebrush mission, vision, values, and staff.

▶ Small group leadership experience for at least one year.

Individual Profile

▶ Seasoned in the church: Has Sagebrush's DNA and feels called to fulfill our vision.

▶ Teachable Spirit: Can take direction and feedback well and has a great desire to learn.

▶ Conflict Resolver: Can handle challenges with Scripture and use Matthew 18 effectively.

▶ Proven Team Leader: Knows how to empower people towards service and excellence.

▶ Excellent Communicator: Can communicate in different areas with clarity and passion.

▶ Healthy Family: Has no concerning spiritual or emotional health issues within family.

▶ Superb Administration Skills: Highly organized and goal oriented personality.

▶ Attention to Detail: Sweats the "small stuff" and pays attention well.

▶ Time Manager: Able to make time for this position to be a priority and adaptable.

▶ Great Personality: Has an engaging, outgoing, people-loving personality.

MULTI-SITE ROADKILL

This book, along with *The Multi-Site Church Revolution*, includes many stories of false starts, dead ends, and downright stupid things that multi-site churches have tried, failed, and learned from, only to continue moving forward. But what about those churches whose multi-site initiative is stuck? What about those who gave up on the multi-site approach and went back to being a single-campus church? Here is our informal, unscientific, nonprioritized list of what we've noticed about multi-site efforts that stalled or died on the side of the road:

1. *Poor choice of campus pastor.* As both our books have emphasized, the role of campus pastor (whatever the person is actually called) is a paramount factor in whether a new campus grows or dies.

2. *Not the senior pastor's vision.* Sometimes the senior pastor never "owned" it, and well-intentioned staff heard a reluctant "Let's see what happens" and took off running. If the new campus doesn't take off quickly, the senior pastor becomes even more unconvinced and unsupportive. Or sometimes there is a change of senior pastors after a new campus is launched, and the new senior pastor wants to take the church in a different direction.

3. *Not the board's vision.* Likewise, sometimes a multi-site initiative dies because the board doesn't really support it, such as in a congregation strongly led by a volunteer elder team.

4. *Not enough preparation time.* Only a few churches can do high-speed transitions to a multi-site approach. Most need

time to process both the idea and its implications. Lack of planning, lead time, and emotional processing has guaranteed failure for some multi-site campuses even though their launch day had a good turnout.

5. *Worship that doesn't match the target population.* Probably the second most influential person at a multi-site campus is the worship leader. This is reflected not just in the heart and warmth conveyed from the stage but also in the type of music selected and the quality level at which it's played.

6. *Bad attitudes within the congregation.* Some multi-sites are actually splinter groups that don't like the senior pastor or don't like newcomers. They formed primarily to fellowship with each other with an attitude of "us four and no more." Church is too much about them, and too little about reaching their friends for Christ.

7. *Inadequate resources.* Becoming a multi-site church can be expensive in terms of time, talent, and treasure. Some churches simply run out of resources before the new campus can grow.

8. *Poor choice of location.* Some churches choose sites too near the original campus. They have asked people to skip attending the tailor-made church building with state-of-the art children's facilities to go to church in a nearby high school building where equipment is set up and torn down every weekend.

What's *your* observation? Join the discussion at our blog, www.multisiteroadtrip.com, and offer your perspective.

DISCUSSION QUESTIONS

Chapter 1: The Multi-Site Variety Pack

1. What do you think is an optimum-size campus to replicate the DNA of *your* church? What's the smallest it could be? The largest it could be?
2. What advantages and disadvantages does that size church present?
3. Which essential ministries should you develop IPODs for?
4. What niche opportunities exist in your community where you could plant a campus?

Chapter 2: The Church Planting versus Campus Launch Dilemma

1. What's your church's historic bias: more toward church planting or more toward campus planting?
2. What would be your next steps in deciding whether to expand, and if so, which model to follow?
3. What are your greatest hesitations about starting a new campus or church?

Chapter 3: Getting Multi-Site into Your Genes

1. If your church moved from being a church *with* multiple campuses to being a church *of* multiple campuses, what adjustments would you need to make in your staffing structure?

2. What essential elements of your church's DNA need to be present in every campus?

3. How can you create a tangible presence of your DNA in each campus?

4. What are the top three issues of transition that you and your team will need to address when you make the shift from a church *with* multiple campuses to a church *of* multiple campuses?

Chapter 4: You Want to Launch a Campus *Where*?

1. What are the potential locations that could be considered as campuses for your church?

2. How does each potential campus location rank in terms of:
   a. Positive community image
   b. Location accessibility
   c. Facility accessibility
   d. Room for growth
   e. Noise tolerance
   f. Purchase/rental price
   g. Room for storage
   h. Other

3. How does the "third place" concept fit within your vision for multi-site?

Chapter 5: Changing Your Community One Campus at a Time

1. What community in your area could benefit from a Dream Center–type campus?

2. What are you already doing to meet the needs of that community?

3. What next steps could you take toward making a bigger impact?

4. Who should carry the vision for this unique outreach?

Chapter 6: Internet Campuses—Virtual or Real Reality?

1. How does your church use the internet? Do you believe that establishing an internet campus would work for your congregation?

2. What "neighborhood" (target group) do you hope to reach with your internet campus?

3. How will you cover the basics of establishing your internet campus, including determination of technology, selection of campus pastor, and clarification of connection process?

Chapter 7: Fun with Technology

1. Reread these quotes: "What new technologies on the horizon could we harness for kingdom use within current fund limitations?" and "What are other churches experimenting with that we might explore, budget permitting, for reaching more people and for making more and better disciples of Jesus Christ?" In response, how can you use technology to better connect your campuses?

2. If you are using or considering using video teaching, what next steps do you need to take to improve the experience?

3. What churches should you be learning from to improve how you harness technology?

Chapter 8: Structure Morphing

1. Is your structure too complicated? Why or why not?

2. Do your leaders have enough freedom within your structure to lead? Explain.

3. How is your structure consistent with your vision?

4. How is your structure designed to accommodate growth?

Chapter 9: Going Global

1. What has been your church's greatest international involvement in recent years?

2. What would be the pros and cons of developing an international campus for your church?

3. Who would need to take the next step in order for your church to have a greater cross-cultural partnership in spreading the gospel?

Chapter 10: Shared Communicator

1. What idea in this chapter was hardest for you to accept? Why?

2. What idea made the most sense? Why?

3. How has your church experimented with shared teaching in the past? What is a likely next step?

Chapter 11: Merger Campuses—No Longer a Bad Idea

1. If you have observed a merger, what was the outcome? What about a restart?

2. Have any churches approached you to ask for help in a way that indicated there might be a possibility of a restart or merger? Are there any churches you should approach? Explain.

3. If you merged with another church, what would be the biggest challenge for your congregation?

Chapter 12: Two—or More—at Once

1. Does your multi-site vision or calling lead you to launch two or more campuses at once? Does God appear to be providing an opportunity to do so?

2. Does your church culture embrace the risk necessary to release people for ministry in a manner that meets the human resource needs of simultaneous launches?

3. Do you have the financial resources necessary to support multiple simultaneous launches?

Chapter 13: Multiplied, Multiple Leaders

1. Does your church have a leadership-rich *culture*? If so, what are its distinguishing marks? If not, what might you do to develop one?
2. What are the current components of your leadership development *structure*? What needs to be added or further developed?
3. Where will you find your next round of "leaders of fifty"?

Chapter 14: Are You Sure This Isn't a Sin?

1. For you, what is the greatest theological argument in support of a multi-site approach?
2. What is the greatest hesitation you hear? How do you respond to it?
3. How has becoming multi-site made you more aligned with your church's biblical mission? Or if you haven't become multi-site yet, how would doing so help your church align better with its mission?

Chapter 15: Grandchildren Already?

1. What's your church's track record toward less control and more diversity as you add new sites?
2. How is reproduction part of the DNA of your multi-site model? If you have more than one campus, are your campus leaders looking to birth new campuses? Why or why not?
3. What are creative ways in which you could quickly fund new campuses?
4. How can you help leaders catch the vision of campuses reproducing campuses?

NOTES

1. Geoff Surratt, Greg Ligon, and Warren Bird, *The Multi-Site Church Revolution* (Grand Rapids, Mich.: Zondervan, 2006), 18.
2. Paul Vitello, "Bad Times Draw Bigger Crowds to Churches," *www.nytimes.com/2008/12/14/nyregion/14churches.html?pagewanted=1&_r=3* (December 14, 2008).
3. Nick More, *http://timestranscript.canadaeast.com/news/article/461194* (October 27, 2008).
4. The survey was conducted December 2008 with 1,004 pastors. In response to the question, 15 percent said yes. There are roughly three hundred thousand Protestant churches in the United States, so 15 percent extrapolates to forty-five thousand churches (Scott McConnell, *Multi-Site Churches* [Nashville: Broadman and Holman, 2009], 3).
5. For more on New Hope's culture, see Robert Lewis, Wayne Cordeiro, and Warren Bird, *Culture Shift* (San Francisco: Jossey Bass, 2005), 79–90.
6. Surratt, Ligon, Bird, *Multi-Site Church Revolution*, 51, 53.
7. Ibid., 38–39, 105.
8. Warren Bird, "Survey of Churches That Worship in Movie Theaters," *www.leadnet.org/papers* (free download; search for keyword *theater*).
9. Ray Oldenburg, *Great Good Place: Cafes, Coffee Shops, Bookstores, Bars, Hair Salons, and Other Hangouts at the Heart of a Community*, 3rd ed. (New York: Marlowe and Company, 1999).
10. Dino Rizzo, *Servolution: Starting a Revolution through Serving* (Grand Rapids, Mich.: Zondervan, 2009).
11. Scott Andron, "Internet Churches: Religious Webcasts Drawing More Congregants," McClatchy newspapers, *www.denverpost.com/technology/ci_7228105* (October 27, 2007).

12. Lyle E. Schaller, "Should We Merge?" *Small Membership Church* (Nashville: Abingdon, 2000), chapter 5.

13. Ronald E. Keener, "City of Grace Becomes One Church, Two Locations—With More to Come," *http://churchexecutive.com/article.asp?IndexID=1155* (January 2009).

14. *http://blogs.lifeway.com/blog/edstetzer/2008/06/questions-for-mcchurch.html*.

15. *www.desiringgod.org/ResourceLibrary/Sermons/ByDate/2007/2479_Treasuring_Christ_Together_as_a_Church_on_Multiple_Campuses/*.

16. Scott McConnell, *Multi-Site Churches: Guidance for the Movement's Next Generation* (Nashville: Broadman and Holman, 2009), 22.

17. *www.leadnet.org/multisite*.

18. *http://blogs.lifeway.com/blog/edstetzer/2008/06/questions-for-questions-for-mc.html*.

SUBJECT INDEX

Written by Shirley Landmesser

Note: page numbers in italics refer to tables.

CHURCH INDEX

Written by Shirley Landmesser

Note: page numbers in italics refer to tables.

ABOUT THE AUTHORS

Geoff Surratt has been on staff at Seacoast Church since 1996, where he has served in almost every role except senior pastor. (He is considering a bloodless coup.) In 2002 he was tasked with pioneering the multi-site effort at Seacoast and has overseen the launch of ten new campuses there since then. He is currently the pastor of ministries, but that could change at any minute. Geoff also worked alongside coauthors Greg and Warren at Leadership Network with the Multi-Site Churches Leadership Communities from 2003 to 2006. He is married to the beautiful and talented Sherry, and they have two wonderful children, one lovely daughter-in-law, and one mangy dog. Geoff's first solo book, *10 Stupid Things That Keep Churches from Growing* (Zondervan), was released in May 2009. He may be reached at GeoffSurratt@seacoast.org.

Greg Ligon has been with Leadership Network since 1997. He currently serves as vice president of church innovations and as publisher. In this role, he oversees several Leadership Community directors and the organization's publishing partnerships. He has also directed the Multi-Site Churches Leadership Community, directed the Leadership Training Network, and spearheaded strategic services for the organization. Additionally, Greg is one of the authors of *The Multi-Site Church Revolution*. For seven years prior to joining Leadership Network, Greg was responsible for creating and directing the United Methodist Campus Ministry at Southern Methodist University in Dallas. He also served as associate pastor at First United Methodist Church in Waco, Texas. Greg and his wife, Susan, have two full-throttle boys, Daniel and Andrew. He may be reached at greg.ligon@leadnet.org.

Warren Bird, PhD, has collaboratively authored twenty-one books (including two one-hundred-thousand-copy bestsellers, one Gold Medallion winner, and one runner-up for the Gold Medallion), served as an assisting pastor for eleven years and senior pastor for four years, taught as regularly contributing faculty at Alliance Theological Seminary for fourteen years, and served on the senior leadership team of three organizations that provide training to pastors—Charles E. Fuller Institute, Canadian Centre for Leadership Development, and the Beeson Institute for Advanced Church Leadership. He is currently research director at Leadership Network, overseeing the creation of a wide range of knowledge products designed to resource church leaders. Warren and his wife, Michelle, live in metro New York City and have two grown children. He may be reached at warren.bird@leadnet.org.

About the Leadership Network Innovation Series

Since 1984, Leadership Network has fostered church innovation and growth by diligently pursuing its far-reaching mission statement: To identify high-capacity Christian leaders, to connect them with other leaders, and to help them multiply their impact.

While specific techniques may vary as the church faces new opportunities and challenges, Leadership Network consistently focuses on bringing together entrepreneurial leaders who are pursuing similar ministry initiatives. The resulting peer-to-peer interaction, dialogue, and collaboration—often across denominational lines—helps these leaders better refine their individual strategies and accelerate their own innovations.

To further enhance this process, Leadership Network develops and distributes highly targeted ministry tools and resources, including books, DVDs and videotapes, special reports, e-publications, and free downloads.

Launched in 2006, the Leadership Network Innovation Series presents case studies and insights from leading practitioners and pioneering churches that are successfully navigating the ever-changing streams of spiritual renewal in modern society. Each book offers *real* stories, about *real* leaders, in *real* churches, doing *real* ministry. Readers gain honest and thorough analyses, transferable principles, and clear guidance on how to put proven ideas to work in their individual settings.

With the assistance of Leadership Network—and the Leadership Network Innovation Series—today's Christian leaders are energized, equipped, inspired, and enabled to multiply their own dynamic kingdom-building initiatives. And the pace of innovative ministry is growing as never before.

For additional information on the mission or activities of Leadership Network, please contact:

LEADERSHIP ✖ NETWORK®

800-765-5323 • www.leadnet.org • client.care@leadnet.org

The Multi-Site Church Revolution

Being One Church in Many Locations

Geoff Surratt, Greg Ligon, and Warren Bird

Read the about the *Revolution* that fueled the *Road Trip*, the first book on multi-site churches by Geoff, Greg and Warren!

The Multi-Site Church Revolution shows what healthy multi-site churches look like and what motivates congregations to make the change.

> "Our multiple-campus approach enables us to reach far more people for Christ, and this book has greatly helped train our staff."
>
> —Craig Groeschel, pastor, LifeChurch.tv

> "I wholeheartedly recommend this book for any pastor or church leader who needs to know the pertinent issues, tested solutions, and real examples of multi-site strategies that are currently being deployed around the world."
>
> —Ed Young, senior pastor, Fellowship Church

> "The authors have done their homework. They have firsthand knowledge of the successes and failures of this movement, having been networking with and facilitating dialogue among churches across the country for years."
>
> —Max Lucado, senior minister, Oak Hills Church

> "Look no further than this book to propel your ministry to Ephesians 3:20 proportions: exceeding abundantly above all that you could ever ask or think!"
>
> —Randy and Paula White, senior pastors, Without Walls International Church

Softcover: 978-0-310-27015-7W

Ethnic Blends

Mixing Diversity into the Local Church

Mark DeYmaz and Harry Li

The local church today stands poised to experience what could be the 21st century's new Reformation: the rise of multi-ethnic churches. Increasingly, church leaders are now recognizing the intrinsic power and beauty of the multi-ethnic church. Yet more than a good idea, it's a biblical, 1st century standard with far-reaching evangelistic potential.

But in a Christian culture where distinctions so often and otherwise divide, how can you and your congregation overcome the obstacles in order to become a healthy, fruitful multi-ethnic church of faith? And why should you even try?

In *Ethnic Blends*, multi-ethnic church pioneer Mark DeYmaz provides an up-close and personal look at seven common challenges to mixing diversity into your local church. Through real-life stories and practical illustrations, DeYmaz shows how to overcome the obstacles in order to build a healthy multi-ethnic church. He also includes the insights of other effective, multi-ethnic local church pastors from around the country.

Softcover: 978-0-310-32123-1

For purchase information, sample chapters and author videos visit www.Zondervan.com/LNIS

Sticky Church

Larry Osborne

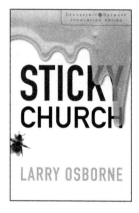

In *Sticky Church*, author and pastor Larry Osborne makes the case that closing the back door of your church is even more important than opening the front door wider. He offers a time-tested strategy for doing so: sermon-based small groups that dig deeper into the weekend message and tightly velcro members to the ministry. It's a strategy that enabled Osborne's congregation to grow from a handful of people to one of the larger churches in the nation—without any marketing or special programming.

Sticky Church tells the inspiring story of North Coast Church's phenomenal growth and offers practical tips for launching your own sermon-based small group ministry. Topics include:

Why stickiness is so important
Why most of our discipleship models don't work very well
Why small groups always make a church more honest and
transparent
What makes groups grow deeper and sticker over time

Sticky Church is an ideal book for church leaders who want to start or retool their small group ministry—and velcro their congregation to the Bible and each other

Softcover: 978-0-310-28508-3

*For purchase information, sample chapters and author videos
visit www.Zondervan.com/LNIS*

The Monkey and the Fish

Liquid Leadership for a
Third-Culture Church

Dave Gibbons

Our world is marked by unprecedented
degrees of multiculturalism, ethnic diversity, social shifts, international collaboration, and technology-driven changes. The
changes are profound, especially when
you consider the unchecked decline in the influence, size, and social standing of the church. There is an undercurrent of anxiety in
the evangelical world, and a hunger for something new. And we're
sensing the urgency of it.

We need fresh, creative counterintuitive ways of doing ministry
and leading the church in the 21st century. We need to adapt. Fast.
Both in our practices and our thinking.

The aim of this book is simple: When we understand the powerful forces at work in the world today, we'll learn how something
called the third culture can yield perhaps the most critical missing
ingredient in the church today—adaptability—and help the church
remain on the best side of history.

A third-culture church and a third-culture leader look at our
new global village and the church's role in that village in a revolutionary way. It's a way to reconnect with the historical roots of
what Jesus envisioned the church could be—a people known for
a brand of love, unity, goodness, and extravagant spirit that defies
all conventions.

This book is part of the successful Leadership Innovation
Series.

Softcover: 978-0-310-27602-9

Deliberate Simplicity

How the Church Does More by Doing Less

Dave Browning

Less is more. And more is better. This is the new equation for church development, a new equation with eternal results.

Rejecting the "bigger is better" model of the complex, corporate megachurch, church innovator Dave Browning embraced deliberate simplicity. The result was Christ the King Community Church, International (CTK), an expanding multisite community church that *Outreach* magazine named among America's Fastest Growing Churches and America's Most Innovative Churches. Members of the CTK network in a number of cities, countries, and continents are empowered for maximum impact by Browning's "less is more" approach.

In *Deliberate Simplicity*, Browning discusses the six elements of this streamlined model:

- Minimality: Keep it simple
- Intentionality: Keep it missional
- Reality: Keep it real
- Multility: Keep it cellular
- Velocity: Keep it moving
- Scalability: Keep it expanding

Part of the Leadership Network Innovation Series

Softcover: 978-0-310-28567-0

The Big Idea

Focus the Message—Multiply the Impact

Dave Ferguson, Jon Ferguson, and Eric Bramlett

Community Christian Church embraced the Big Idea and everything changed. They decided to avoid the common mistake of bombarding people with so many "little ideas" that they suffered overload. They also recognized that leaders often don't insist that the truth be lived out to accomplish Jesus' mission. Why? Because people's heads are swimming with too many little ideas, far more than they can ever apply.

The Big Idea can help you creatively present one laser-focused theme each week to be discussed in families and small groups. It shows how to engage in a process of creative collaboration that brings people together and maximizes missional impact. *The Big Idea* can energize a church staff and bring alignment and focus to diverse church ministries.

This book shows how the Big Idea has helped Community Christian Church better accomplish the Jesus mission and reach thousands of people in nine locations and launch a church planting network with partner churches across the country.

Softcover: 978-0-310-27241-0

For purchase information, sample chapters and author videos visit www.Zondervan.com/LNIS

Leadership Network Innovation Series

LNIS Sampler - February 2009

real stories | innovative ideas | transferrable truths

One chapter from each current Leadership Network Innovation Series titles.

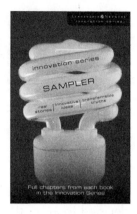

How can you fulfill your calling as a church leader and help your church experience vitality?

One way is by learning from those that have gone before you: church leaders who are successfully navigating the ever-changing streams of spiritual renewal in modern society. In partnership with Leadership Network, Zondervan presents the Leadership Network Innovation Series. These books are real stories, about real leaders, in real churches doing real ministry—the ups and downs and the practical helps for doing innovative and culture-changing ministry. Each story features transferable principles and provides guidance on how you can apply these principles within your own ministry context.

For purchase information, sample chapters and author videos visit www.Zondervan.com/LNIS

ZONDERVAN®
.com